MICHAEL FINNEY'S CONSUMER CONFIDENTIAL

Michael Finney's
CONSUMER
CONFIDENTIAL

The Money-Saving Secrets
They Don't Want You to Know

Michael Finney

BK

BERRETT-KOEHLER PUBLISHERS, INC.
San Francisco

Berrett-Koehler Publishers, Inc.
235 Montgomery Street, Suite 650
San Francisco, CA 94104-2916
Tel: (415) 288-0260   Fax: (415) 362-2512   www.bkconnection.com

ORDERING INFORMATION
QUANTITY SALES. Special discounts are available on quantity purchases by corporations, associations, and others. For details, contact the "Special Sales Department" at the Berrett-Koehler address above.
INDIVIDUAL SALES. Berrett-Koehler publications are available through most bookstores. They can also be ordered directly from Berrett-Koehler:
Tel: (800) 929-2929; Fax: (802) 864-7626; www.bkconnection.com
ORDERS FOR COLLEGE TEXTBOOK/COURSE ADOPTION USE. Please contact Berrett-Koehler:
Tel: (800) 929-2929; Fax: (802) 864-7626.
ORDERS BY U.S. TRADE BOOKSTORES AND WHOLESALERS. Please contact Publishers Group West, 1700 Fourth Street, Berkeley, CA 94710. Tel: (510) 528-1444; Fax (510) 528-3444.

Berrett-Koehler and the BK logo are registered trademarks of Berrett-Koehler Publishers, Inc.

Printed in the United States of America

Berrett-Koehler books are printed on long-lasting acid-free paper. When it is available, we choose paper that has been manufactured by environmentally responsible processes. These may include using trees grown in sustainable forests, incorporating recycled paper, minimizing chlorine in bleaching, or recycling the energy produced at the paper mill.

Library of Congress Cataloging-in-Publication Data
Finney, Michael, 1956
      Michael Finney's consumer confidential : the money-saving secrets they don't want you to know / by Michael Finney
      p.cm.
      Includes bibliographical references and index.
      ISBN 1-57675-300-X
      1. Finance, Personal   I. Title: Consumer confidential.   II. Title.
HG179.F5313 2004
332.024—dc22   20040466297

First Edition
08 07 06 05 04   10 9 8 7 6 5 4 3 2 1

Text design by Dianne Platner.

For my brother, Bob. He taught me how
the world worked and how the world *should* work.

Contents

Acknowledgments

No one is more responsible for this book than Kevin Keeshan. Among the nation's finest broadcast journalists, and long time consumer advocate, Kevin encouraged me to become a full time consumer reporter in the first place. He has held my reporting and advocacy to the highest of standards ever since. Sometimes that is irritating; it is always enlightening.

Without the support of Valari Staab, the General Manager of KGO-TV, and Mickey Luckoff, the General Manager of KGO-AM, my reporting could never have had the far-reaching impact that it has enjoyed. Mickey and Valari are the very best this industry has to offer.

Greg Tantum, Dan Ashley, Paul Sands, Gene Ross, Milt Weiss, and Jim Topping have all been crucial; each knows why. Greg Hunter you were wonderful, as always. To members of the 'Three Forward Thinking Dudes', I thank you for allowing me to join your exclusive club.

Carol Susan Roth is my agent, my friend, and a fine provocateur; this book reflects her vision of the world as much as mine. I appreciate everyone at Berrett-Koehler Publishers for being so kind to this newbie. Steve and Jeevan have been especially patient. I can't thank them enough.

Finally my family, where do I begin? My mother, Nancy Finney, can return anything anywhere and leave everyone laughing. She is the best consumer I know. My father, Robert Finney, is the epitome of the strong silent type. He taught me ethical behavior through his actions and words. Brenda held my hand throughout the process of writing this book and throughout the process of life. Connor and Kelly constantly remind me why all of this is so important.

To those I left out, pardon me.

Introduction: Learning the Hard Way

I still remember the feeling vividly. Wind in my face, pedaling hard, weaving back and forth across the street. Using a sidearm technique, which I was quite sure I had invented, I threw newspapers the way other kids skipped stones. The perfect throw was when the paper gently landed on the stoop, but with enough force behind it to slide up to the welcome mat.

That was the good part of paperboying: that Zen-like feeling of being at one with the elements, the bicycle, and the newspaper. The not-so-good part was nearly everything else. By signing on as a newspaper boy, I had taken a front-row seat in a classroom at the school of hard knocks. The customers didn't want to pay their bills, much less tip. The newspaper company always wanted more for less.

When you are working every day and have an income of $32 a month, even at 11 years old you have a deep understanding that you are on the bottom rung of the employment ladder. From that rung you look up, both literally and figuratively, to all your clients and bosses. It's a perspective that still deeply affects me today.

As in any endeavor, it's the best and worst that you remember years later. My oldest customer was my favorite; he always treated me with great respect and paid on time. He never missed an opportunity to remark, "Mike, what a fine young man you are growing up to be." He lived on the top floor of an old two-story farmhouse. I could have thrown his paper on the bottom step but never did. Every day, I got off my Sting-Ray, walked halfway up the steps, and threw the paper on his welcome mat. I felt privileged to be his paperboy.

Down the street from him was a well-to-do family that rented a home and was a constant hassle. A classic example was the time the woman of the house telephoned, interrupting my dinner, to say that a paper hadn't been delivered. Her house had a carport directly in front of the door, so I asked if it was possible that someone had parked on top of the paper. She angrily replied no and demanded that a paper be brought to her right that minute. I left the dinner table and pedaled over to the house, where she waited, fuming, at her front door. "What took you so long?" She was one ticked-off woman.

I crawled under the car, where the newspaper lay. I crawled back out and handed the woman her paper. She snatched it from my hand and without saying a word shut the door in my face. She had been lazy and rude...because I was young and little.

I knew right then that she could not be trusted. After that incident, I always collected payment from her on the 25th of each month. Payment wasn't due until the 30th, but I now knew that she would move without paying me and never give it a thought. Since most families move on the last day of the month, I wasn't going to give her a chance to skip out on her bill.

Being a newspaper boy taught me to think about what could go wrong and how to protect myself. It also taught me how to negotiate for what I wanted. After I was on the job for a few months, I felt that I deserved more money. My paper route was a difficult one, with several major streets to cross and a business district. I used that information to negotiate a raise. I wanted 20 cents more per customer, the newspaper offered 10 cents, and we settled on 15 cents. My income increased to $42 a month.

Several months later an easier, better-paying paper route became available, so I applied for it. The district manager said he wouldn't give it to me because it would be too tough to replace me on my current route. I used that information to negotiate another raise, and my income increased to $48 a month.

By becoming a smarter consumer, I was able to make even more money. I found a local bakery that would sell me its misprinted plastic bags for about half of what the newspaper charged me for its rainy-day bags. I found a wholesaler that beat the newspaper's price on rubber bands. Now my monthly income was $52.

My experience as a newspaper boy set up the rest of my life. Here are the most important things I learned all those years ago:

- Trust everyone until they do you wrong; then watch them closely.
- When negotiating, be fair and know what you want.
- There is always a cheaper place to buy anything.
- The cross-body sidearm Finney Pitch is the only correct way to throw a newspaper.

The Basics

Chapter 1

What is a Good Consumer?

"**d**o you get what you pay for?" That is the best consumer question I have ever been asked, and I have been asked a lot of consumer questions. I have answered thousands in my television reports, during my radio talk show, and in newspaper columns. "Do you get what you pay for?"

My answer? You get what you *ask* for. If you are trying to show off to impress friends or strangers, rest assured, you will overpay. If you are trying to be the cheapest human being alive, you'll surely get an item similar to what you want—but not the real thing—less expensively.

Being a good consumer is not about money, it's about awareness and fairness. A good consumer is aware of his or her surroundings, legally and emotionally. Good consumers are concerned about what is fair, for others as well as themselves.

Far too many people equate consumerism with money. Certainly money and consumerism run parallel courses, but they are not one and the same.

I disagree with my consumer-activist colleagues on most money issues. They have been taught, and pass along, the concept that money is the root of all evil; many even believe that money itself is evil. Too often my peers are obsessed with money, either pushing it away or hoarding it. They carry a strange dichotomy of thought: on one hand, money is evil and should be avoided; on the other hand, money is too precious to spend, so it must be piled up and guarded at all costs. Which is it? Neither! Both of these thoughts are toxic. Money is a means to an end—that's it.

Other consumer activists I know spout the individual-above-all doctrine, saying in their oh-so-sly way that anything you can "pull off" is good. Find a new way to rip off a major company and you are a hero. Slip through a government loophole and you are to be congratulated. For these people, life is like a caper movie—say, *Ocean's 11*—only on a smaller scale. Not me. Just as being cheap doesn't make you a good consumer, in my book, being slimy doesn't work either.

Consumerism = fairness

Consumerism is a lifestyle choice that puts personal worth above personal wealth. Being a good consumer means going after what is fair for you and for others. It's about finding your own comfort zone and your own place in this world, while freely allowing others their space and breathing room. Being a good consumer means being a good person and gently nudging others to join in.

A woman called me while she was going through some terrible times with her insurance company. She had had a fire in her home, and the company seemed to be doing everything in its power not to offer a fair settlement. She had complained and argued and was now simply worn out. "Michael," she said, "I've paid my premiums for years and shouldn't have to go through this—the company should do what is right."

I contacted the insurance company and asked for a review of the case. Knowing that I was keeping track of its shenanigans, the company sent a new adjuster to the home, and the consumer was offered a much higher settlement.

The burned-out bedroom was indeed rebuilt, and the company was there every step of the way, making sure that everything was getting done correctly. The woman was thrilled, and the company avoided bad press. A win-win, but there was still more to do. I telephoned the company's CEO.

He said, "We've done everything you want. The house is rebuilt; our client is thrilled." He was annoyed. "What more do you want?"

I said, "We want an apology."

"What?"

"Your client needs an apology. Sure, you paid what you owed, but that's simply doing what you were supposed to do. You never said you were sorry."

The phone line went silent; I could hear breathing, so I waited. Probably 15 or 20 seconds went by without either of us saying a word.

Then the CEO said, "To me it was business; to her it was personal." You could all but hear the idea sinking in. "You are right, we owe her an apology."

Later that day he personally called the woman and apologized. Now that is a consumer victory! Education occurred—possibly even personal growth.

The Seven Steps to Winning Every Consumer Argument

1. Respect yourself

Whether you are trying to return a $20 blouse you bought one week ago or a $20,000 car you bought one year ago, the process is remarkably the same. It all begins with respect.

You must respect yourself enough to go after what is right. Many consumers just shrug off lousy treatment time after time. After a while they are programmed to be a victim. How does this happen? It generally begins in childhood. We all carry with us our life story. It's like a guidebook to our personal selves and how we react to any given situation.

If as a child you were told often enough by your parents to be quiet, you may learn to keep your thoughts to yourself even into adulthood. If bullies stole your lunch money, you may get used to, and even expect, a certain level of economic violence. If older siblings took advantage of your good nature and grabbed two pieces of bubble gum when you only offered one, you were programmed to expect fraud and deceit.

We all have a victimization chapter in our books, and, making matters worse, we tend to read those chapters out loud when in the marketplace. We broadcast our victimhood when buying a stereo or complaining about a lousy haircut. Those we are dealing with pick up on the victim vibe.

Two perfect examples: a guy buying a new suit and a woman entering a car lot. You've heard these stories a hundred times. The clothing saleswoman talks in circles about materials and cuts that the man doesn't understand, while the car salesman talks about mechanics and sound systems the woman couldn't care less about (of course, it could be the other way around, too). It's not a coincidence; salespeople are professionals at reading the victim vibe.

So the first step to solving a consumer problem is to put the personal history aside and start this day as a new one. You deserve respect, so expect it. When complaining about a consumer issue, smile and say hello. If you are complaining in person, don't slouch. If you are complaining in a phone call, don't mumble. Act and talk as if you complain about consumer issues all the time and always get what you want.

Keep your past as a consumer victim a secret. Play down the past often enough, and as time goes on, you'll have new headings in your victimhood chapter—headings like "The Time I Complained," "How I Stood Up for Myself," and, finally, "Winning with a Consumer Complaint."

Your victim chapter can become your power chapter.

2. Know what you want

No child ever sat on Santa Claus's lap and didn't know what she or he wanted. Few employees have ever gone in to ask for a raise without having a dollar figure in mind. Yet consumers complain all the time about issues without having any idea how they want things to play out.

I had a consumer once call in to my radio show about a lemon car.

"It has never worked correctly," she told me. "Six months after I bought it, the car was in the shop for two weeks and has been back in the shop five times since then, and it's only been three months. It still doesn't run right."

"What do you want done?" I asked. "What would be a fair solution?"

She told me she hadn't really thought about that. "How about a promise to keep fixing the car even after the warranty expires?"

Now that was a little like going off to college proclaiming that you are going to get all Cs. It might be OK, but you should aim a little higher, and that's what I told this consumer. "Look, why don't you ask for a new car. The law says you can return this one and, minus a small mileage charge, get your money back."

She liked the idea and eventually, with the help of an attorney, returned the car and got a refund.

Before complaining, know what you want, and be ready to say it with good humor. A few years back, I was vacationing on the beach and rented snorkeling gear. There were signs everywhere saying that if equipment was damaged, the consumer had to pay for a replacement.

I went snorkeling and, of course, ripped a fin while taking it off. When I returned it, I pointed out the damage, and the clerk told me it would cost me fifty bucks.

I said, "No way am I paying that."

He said, "There's the sign—we were clear on what would happen."

"Yes," I said, "you were clear on the concept, but not the cost or my situation." He asked what I meant.

I said, "First of all, you are charging me retail, when you

are going to buy wholesale; at most a new set will cost you $25 a pair." The clerk was a sharp guy and said, "OK, give me $25 and we'll call it even."

Because I had given some thought to what I wanted and what this conversation was going to be like, I was ready with a response. "That's not fair," I said. "I only ripped one fin, so that cuts the cost in half."

The clerk was a little taken aback but said, "OK, I have never done this before, but give me $12.50 and we'll call it even."

I said, "No, that's not fair either."

He was getting frustrated and asked why.

"These fins are old—that's why they ripped," I told him. "You have rented these many times, and the fins are worn out because of all that wear and tear."

The snorkel guy was ready to get rid of me, so he said, "How about six bucks?"

Now I must admit that getting the charge down to $6 from $50 is pretty good, but I wasn't ready to throw in the towel just yet. "Look, if I pay you the $6, I'll feel ripped off."

He was at the end of his rope and asked, "What is it you want?"

That was the question I was waiting to hear, the one I was prepared to answer. "I want to leave here feeling good about my day at the beach, so that next year I'll come back and rent snorkeling gear from you again."

The clerk looked at the growing line behind me and said, "Mr. Finney, I'll see you next summer."

Knowing what I wanted and explaining why I should have it got the job done for me, and it can get the job done for you as well.

3. Be flexible and ready to negotiate

Although you need to know what you want, don't assume

that's the only solution to your problem. True, I didn't want to pay for the ripped fin, but I might have paid the $6 if I had been given a half-off coupon for the next time I rented snorkeling gear. There could have been other solutions; the important thing is to stay flexible.

Negotiating is an important part of the business and legal professions. It is also important to anyone trying to buy a chair at a garage sale or an expensive piece of art at a big-city gallery.

There are hundreds of books and thousands of typed pages devoted to the subject, but the best advice on negotiating I ever heard came from the wife of a deceased Mafia deal maker. The underworld figure had actually died in his 80s of natural causes. He had lived a long life, his wife said, because he understood that everyone at the table had to get a piece of the pie. He may have been a criminal, but he knew not to take more than his fair share. He made sure that everyone walked away with what was most important to him or her.

If that philosophy can keep an organized-crime boss alive for 80 years, it truly has something to offer all of us. Keep in mind the other person's agenda.

4. Give everyone a chance to do the right thing

This rule is so important for consumers to keep in mind because it ends many problems just as they are starting. By giving everyone the benefit of the doubt, you put yourself in a better position. Start with what is easy, and work your way to hard.

I learned this when I bought my first car. One day the engine wouldn't turn over; there was no power at all. I figured that it wasn't the starter, since there was no sound, so I was looking at the alternator as the source of the problem. I was working hundreds of miles from home that summer and had a mechanic look at the car. He agreed with me and suggested that I install a new alternator. I called my father for a second opinion, and he said, "Why not try the battery?"

I asked why, and he said, "Because that's the cheapest and easiest thing to replace." I bought a new battery, which fixed the problem and gave me a new mantra: start easy and work your way to hard. That's true when repairing a car, working on a relationship, or filing a consumer complaint.

Assume the right thing will be done, and often that's the way things work out, so you don't have to get all stressed. Give everyone the chance to do the right thing. Start easy.

5. Don't respond in anger

If the "easy" doesn't occur, be ready to take it up a notch. However, do so calmly and with dignity. I often mediate problems that could easily have been solved by a supervisor—and would have been, if only the consumer had gotten through to one. The consumer often doesn't, because in the company's computer files tracking the complaint, he or she has been red-flagged as being uncooperative or angry.

Recently I had problems with a telephone clerk for a major credit card company. Actually, it was more than a problem—the clerk hung up on me. I called the number back and the operator answering the phone identified herself as Debbie. I thanked Debbie for her time and asked to speak to a supervisor. She told me that wasn't possible. I told her, "Debbie, I am calling to complain about an operator just like you. At this moment I don't have a problem with you or your work, but if I am not connected with a supervisor soon, you are going to be added to my complaint list."

I was telling the truth; Debbie knew it, and she connected me with a supervisor right away.

I was angry but didn't allow myself to become the issue. The issue was poor customer service, not my reaction to it. I kept the focus on the real problem by not directly responding to the first operator's rudeness or to Debbie's lack of concern.

6. Take the high road

A big mistake consumers make every day is to start citing laws and talking about lawyers. "I'll sue—you'll hear from my attorney," they say to a clerk in a major department store. By saying that, they have boxed themselves into a corner, a very small legal corner. You see, when a consumer talks about what she can do legally to a store, the government, or a service provider, she has confined the conversation to a very small arena.

Never talk about what is legal; talk about what is moral. Talk about what is fair and what has occurred in the past. By and large, talking about anything but what is legal works best for consumers. Here's why: businesses know more about the law than you do and often employ huge numbers of lawyers to interpret the law and huge numbers of lobbyists to help create the laws.

Now ask yourself, who has better legal standing, you or an entire industry? Even if the answer is you, you probably don't have the money or stamina to make your legal point stick. So instead talk about how good the company has acted in the past; talk about how it could lose a customer; talk about going to the media; talk about going to Michael Finney and how that could hurt its business. Don't talk about what is legal unless you are a lawyer or really are willing to sue.

7. Be ready to do battle

If you can't get the business to budge or you are dealing with a criminal enterprise—say, a mechanic who set out to rip you off—be ready to do battle. That means you'll be taking time out of your day to complain to the district attorney's office, consumer advocacy groups, and state agencies. Be ready to find an attorney and/or to file a small claims court action. Going to court is more energy-consuming than most people know and is seldom worth the effort. But winning in court, on the other hand, is also a better feeling than most people know, and it makes a legal fight somewhat appealing if you feel mistreated enough, if you feel put-upon enough, if "enough is enough."

How to Write a Complaint Letter

don't be a crazy person. That is the number one rule for writing a complaint letter. I'm not kidding—that simple idea will go a long way toward getting your problem resolved. It's simple: If you come across as having your act together, you have a good shot at getting the complaint dealt with quickly. If, on the other hand, you come across as out of control, your letter will be ignored.

As a consumer reporter I receive more than 1,000 consumer complaints a week. I have been on the job for well over a decade. Do the math. I have read thousands upon thousands of lousy complaint letters and a handful of good ones. Here's what I've learned:

By the time most consumers are ready to sit down and write a complaint letter, they are fed up. They also know every single detail by heart. The problem has taken on gigantic proportions—if not in real life, then in the consumer's mind. This is completely understandable. The consumer feels wronged and has worked hard to get the problem solved. Yet nothing is resolved. Because of that, consumers end up writing exactly the wrong complaint letter: a letter that is too long and too complex.

Advice

If you must CC your letter, CC it to only one organization. Although most consumers are convinced that it helps to CC a letter to a host of agencies and individuals, it does not help. Usually it shows that you are an amateur. Those of us who receive CCs tend to ignore them. If the letter is being CC'ed to a half-dozen organizations, I assume that everyone else is reading the CC and I can ignore it guilt-free.

One consumer wrote me a letter about her experience with a leaking faucet. She wrote about the decision to buy a new sink. How she had shopped for a faucet. Why she had bought the faucet she'd decided upon. How much the faucet had cost and the store where she had made the purchase.

She explained how the faucet was installed and who installed it. She described her mistreatment by the company that made the faucet. Whom she spoke with when she complained and what she was told. She explained, in detail, why she felt the customer service representative was snide.

The letter went on for ten pages before she stated the problem: the faucet leaked. In journalism that's called *burying the lead*. That's when the most important fact—the faucet leaked—is overwhelmed by less important facts.

Because the consumer had been dealing with the problem for so long, she knew too much. If you find yourself in a similar situation, here's all you need to know to write a complaint letter that will get read and acted upon.

1. You get four paragraphs—that's it. No more, no matter how complex the problem. This letter may be the first in a series of contacts; you will offer more information later, if requested, but you cannot force it down their throats.

2. The paragraphs must be short and to the point.

3. Don't be snide or condescending.

4. Don't complain about the complaint process. That is a different letter.

Advice

Don't send a letter addressed to a major corporation and expect a response. The letter must be addressed to a specific person. Telephone or go online and look for the name of the person in charge of complaints, or at least the person in charge of the product or service you are complaining about. If you can't find the division manager's name or the consumer-complaint person's name, then send the letter to the president of the company, using his or her first and last names in the salutation.

I called the woman with the leaking faucet and suggested that she rewrite the letter into my four-paragraph style. She took my advice, and the company took care of her problem.

E-mail is an easy way to complain, and that's why e-mails tend to get ignored. With e-mail, consumers don't have to put forth much effort to write the complaint. In return, companies don't put forth much effort to fix the problem. The more you put out, the more you get back. Don't expect some company employee to jump through hoops to solve your problem when you aren't even willing to stamp a letter.

A shorter letter is easier to write, and here's your proof.

Sample Complaint Letter

Sally Smith
Director of Consumer Services
XYZ Company
123 Main Street
Anywhere, CA 94111

Dear Ms. Smith:

I am writing to complain about a recent problem I have had with a faucet manufactured by your company. It is the Aireator 5000gf.

The faucet was installed in August 2003 by a professional plumber and worked wonderfully for 12 months. In September 2004, the faucet began leaking while I was out of town traveling. Water damage occurred.

The faucet comes with a "No questions asked" lifetime guarantee, and that is why I am requesting that XYZ pay the costs associated with the damage caused by your faucet.

My total out-of-pocket expenses came to $854.00, as you can see by the attached receipts. I look forward to hearing from you within two weeks.

Sincerely yours,

Your Money

Chapter 2

Credit Counseling

by now, everyone has seen the commercials for debt-service companies that claim to be able to "get you out of debt." If you think you are in financial trouble now, just wait till some of these companies are done with you! What used to be a sure bet for consumers has become a sucker's bet for thousands.

A good credit counselor can help you get out of debt and move ahead with your life; others, though, aren't there to help you but to help themselves to your money. This industry has changed dramatically.

It wasn't long ago that most areas had only one debt-counseling service. Often called Consumer Credit Counseling Service (CCCS), it was a respected locally run nonprofit enterprise. Counselors with the CCCS would help consumers get out of debt by helping them set up a workable budget and then negotiating new payment plans with lenders. Often the interest rate would be cut and the monthly minimum payment would be lowered, and sometimes a portion of the debt itself would be forgiven.

Consumers would write a check to the CCCS, and the counselors would send out their payments. It was a win-win situation. Companies were repaid and retained their customers. Consumers got out of debt without filing for bankruptcy. The consumer sometimes paid a minimal fee to the CCCS, and lenders picked up the rest of the tab. Many CCCSs still operate that way, although the fees, in some areas, are creeping up. Now the CCCSs have competition. Some new nonprofits and for-profits are heavily advertising in the media, telling consumers they can get out of debt quickly and forever. Consumers report that some of these companies have been a great help while others have been no help at all.

Many of these new debt-relief companies are run by rip-off artists, accused by consumer activists and law enforcement as being wolves in sheep's clothing. Some trick consumers into handing over their paychecks, but none of the money reaches the lender. Once the police get on to the scheme, these credit pirates close up shop, turn off their phones, and head out of town. Later they set up the same business in a new location and find new suckers to rip off.

Before getting involved with any counseling service, make sure you really need the help. Many consumers simply don't want to make their payments, even though they can afford them. If that sounds like your situation, you are *not* a candidate for counseling. You ran up the bills—quit whining and pay them off. If you wish, try to lower your payments by calling lenders and attempting to negotiate a lower interest rate. Just the threat of closing your account and moving to another company is often enough to get an 18 percent credit card interest rate dropped to 10 or 11 percent.

If you can't afford to make the payments, then a credit counseling service might be a good move, but don't sign up with the company making the extravagant claim you want to hear. Just because someone tells you he can settle a $5,000 credit card bill for fifty bucks doesn't mean he can actually do it. Avoid big talkers when looking for debt services.

Many lenders are fed up with counseling services and don't want to deal with them, so you might be able to negotiate a better deal on your own. The important thing is to stop overspending and come up with a plan. If it sounds legitimate to your lenders, you'll often find you can make a deal that will get you out of debt within a few years.

Stop Payment on a Check

Stopping payment on a check is

A. a good way to keep a rip-off artist from taking your money without delivering the goods;

B. a good way to set yourself up for arrest and jail time; or

C. all of the above.

If you picked C, you have a better understanding of our banking system than 90 percent of the consumers out there. Many consumers see putting a "stop" on a check as a catchall when things aren't going their way. A "stopped check" is seen as a good means of leveling the playing field...any playing field.

If your contractor takes money and never does the job, stop payment on the check you wrote to get the work done. If you buy a window air conditioner and it doesn't work, put a stop on the check.

The advice being passed from consumer to consumer is to "stop payment" if you don't like what is going on. Here's the problem with that advice: often the consumer is breaking the law. For instance, if you write a check knowing that you plan to stop payment on it, you may be breaking the law. If your contractor installed all the windows as promised but did a lousy job, and you stop the check, you are most likely breaking the law.

Warning

Stopping payment on a check is not cheap. Call your bank, and you'll find that the average charge can be $35 or more. Stopped-check fees are a good source of income for financial institutions. There is also paperwork to be filled out, so most of the time the consumer either has to go into a bank branch or file the paperwork online.

You can always legally stop payment on a check when it is missing, lost, or stolen. You may also stop payment on a check in case of fraud or misrepresentation, and there's the rub. What is fraud? A lousy job may be fraudulent; it may also just be a lousy job. In this country it's legal to be bad at what you do.

If the air conditioner works but just not well enough to cool the entire room, it's probably not legal to stop payment.

Rarely are charges filed, and more rarely still will a district attorney go after a consumer who feels wronged. However, keep in mind that by stopping a check you have taken an aggressive action, and the individual who tried to cash the check is not going to be happy. A better way to protect yourself is to buy with a credit card, or pay after you receive and inspect goods and services.

Warning

Here's a secret few consumers know: Putting a "stop" on a check is actually more like putting the brakes on a check. A stop on a payment does not last forever. A consumer-placed stop lasts only six months, so if you are concerned that the check could be cashed after that time, you must renew the stop. Of course, there is a fee for that service.

Stupid Card Tricks

Credit card companies keep coming up with new ways to make money, each one more underhanded than the next. One of them involves changing the date when your payment is due. Companies have figured out that consumers get in a pattern and quit reading the due date, so they move up the date a couple of days, and voilà—they get to charge you more interest and a late payment.

Another trick making the rounds: changing the amount of time given consumers to pay their bills, from 30 days to 25 days to 20 days. Again, consumers aren't keeping close track, but the credit card company is.

Zero percent initial financing for new customers is a big selling point these days. These 9- to 12-month interest-free offers can be a great deal, but some of these deals turn consumers into suckers.

A while back, I was remodeling my home and had the money sitting in a bank account, but I thought, why pay all at once when I could get an interest-free loan from a credit card company?

Being a serial card switcher can get you
out of debt. More than one consumer
has contacted me with a success story of
applying for zero percent introductory
offers, paying down their balance a bit,
and then moving on to another zero
percent card. Those successful with this
strategy might go through several cards
before getting the account balance down
to zero. This is a workable plan for
disciplined consumers, but there are
pitfalls. Some zero percent offers charge
a 3 percent fee for balance transfers, and
having too many open credit card
accounts will lower your credit score.
Before going this route, read the fine
print and make sure you won't just run
up new bills.

So I responded to two zero percent credit card offers I'd
received in the mail. Once my applications were accepted, I
transferred about $20,000 to each card. And what were my
monthly payments? On one credit card, $1,400 a month—
about triple what I would normally expect to pay. The second card gave me a minimum payment of $15 a month.

The high-minimum card company either was trying to
ensure that I would be debt-free when the zero percent offer
came to an end or was trying to get me into a financial bind
so that I couldn't make the minimum monthly payment. You
decide which of the two options you believe was occurring.
The other card company, I'm convinced, was banking on the

fact that I would make the $15 payments for a year, leaving me with a huge balance when the zero percent offer ended.

I never paid a dime in interest on either card.

Watch out for cards that say "fixed rate." None of them are *really* fixed. By law, with little notice, the card company can charge you more. As long as the cardholder is notified—and that can be with a small slip of paper that's stuffed into your monthly bill—your interest rate can be upped with 30 days' notice.

Warning

Many consumers are finding that their interest rate on one credit card is being increased because they paid another credit card bill late. This is called *universal default* and is perfectly legal; however, in New York there is a move to make universal defaults against the law. Computerization has allowed credit card companies to keep close track of their customers and to craft interest rates for each one according to how they handle their bills. This ability works for consumers at times but nearly always causes problems if a single credit card payment is made late.

The credit card companies that offer mileage, money back, or other perks usually charge a higher-than-average interest rate or an annual fee, sometimes both. Using these cards can be fun and profitable, but make sure that if you carry a balance, you switch it to a lower-rate card.

With air miles worth about 2.5 cents each, you have to charge at least $3,000 just to break even if you pay a $60 annual fee. Some cards are now coming without annual fees, and others offer a mileage program that isn't tied to a particular airline. Those cards are often a better deal for consumers who aren't frequent fliers with a particular airline.

A while back, I reported on two major credit card companies that seemed to have a problem making deposits. Consumers complained that even though they made their payments on time, the banks did not credit their accounts on time. Sometimes the check would be cashed days before the due date, and still the banks would tack a late fee onto the account.

The federal government got involved, and as of this writing there are no reports of major problems with any banks' crediting accounts. That could change tomorrow, however, so keep close track of when you mail in your payments.

How do you find the credit card that's best for you? A good place to start is with Consumer Action (CA). This San Francisco-based nonprofit provides an extensive credit card survey that is available at www.consumer-action.org. Consumer Action will also mail you a printed copy of the report if you send in a stamped (60 cents), self-addressed envelope to the following address:

Consumer Action

Attn.: Credit Card Survey

717 Market Street, Suite 310

San Francisco, CA 94103-2109

Information

Consumer Action takes on just about any consumer issue, from investments to utilities. Executive Director Ken McEldowney and Editorial Director Linda Sherry, as well as the rest of the staff, do an incredible job of reaching out to the community. CA's publications are available in Chinese, English, Korean, Russian, Spanish, Vietnamese, and other languages.

Credit Report vs. Credit Score

there is a lot of confusion these days about what makes up a credit report and what makes up a credit score. Your credit report is what actually happened: when and where you applied for credit, whom you borrowed money from, and whom you still owe. The report also says if you have paid off a debt and whether you make your monthly payments on time.

A *credit report* is like your little credit paw prints in the snow. Although the reports look confusing to those not used to reading them, they generally are pretty straightforward documents.

Under a new federal law, all three major credit reporting agencies that keep track of you will have to mail you a free credit report each year. You also have the right to get a free report if you have been turned down for credit. If you want additional reports, you must pay for them, and they cost about eight bucks each.

A *credit score* is much more important these days than a credit report. The report offers the raw data that a company crafts into a credit score. Fair Isaac Corporation was the first to come up with a credit score, and that's why you may have heard these scores referred to as *FICO scores*.

Warning

Credit-repair scams take in thousands of consumers every year. The promoters offer to "fix" your credit. That is not possible. If the information in your credit report is wrong, you or someone else can complain and have the information corrected, but you can't repair bad credit. To get a better credit history, live a better credit life by paying your bills on time and not going deeply into debt.

Information

Collection accounts remain on your record for seven years. Although most consumers believe that seven years begins when the missed payment is reported to the collection agency, that's not true. The seven years begins the day of your first missed payment. Credit reporting agencies are allowed to report positive information for as long as they want, so home or car loan payments made on time could, theoretically, go back 20 years. Negative information, like payments you missed, may stay on your report for seven years. Bankruptcies have a shelf life of 10 years, and unpaid tax liens can be reported for 15 years.

Credit scores look at how much credit you have available and how much you are currently using, and they compare that information with your past record and the records of others like you. Having too many department store credit cards lowers your score. If you have just one bank card but it has a high credit limit, that could hurt your score, too. Other variables: the balance you are carrying versus the credit availability, and how many times you have run up huge credit card bills.

The FICO scores range from 500 to 850. If your score is hovering around 500, you'll have a tough time getting a loan, and the money you borrowed will come with a hefty interest rate. If you have a score of 720 or above, you'll receive the best rates available. You get a different score from each of the three major reporting agencies, so the accuracy of each report is important.

Insider Secret

Those folks who have a high credit score tend to be competitive and want to know why their score isn't perfect. The answer is, it doesn't matter. Any score above 720 is enough to get you a great deal on any loan you take out, so don't stress just because you don't have a perfect score—almost no one does, and as it turns out, most lenders don't much like those folks, anyway. People with 850 scores are *so* good that lenders know they're not going to make much money off of them.

Fair Isaac estimates that a person with a score of 550 could get a 30-year mortgage; however, at a time when that consumer's interest rate was hovering at 9.5 percent, someone else with a score above 720 would be looking at an interest rate of 6.5 percent—a 3-point spread. Whether rates go up or down, the spread stays pretty much the same.

Not long ago, the company treated your credit score like a state secret. You couldn't even have access to it. Fair Isaac refused to say how the score was arrived at—but not now.

Now the company has a much more open attitude and has created a Web site, myFICO (www.myfico.com), where for less than $15 you can get a single credit report and the score attached to that report. For just less than $40 you can get reports from all three major reporting agencies and your credit score attached to each of those reports. If you plan to set up a cell phone account or buy a car, the cheaper of the two options will probably be fine. If you plan to buy a house, order all three reports and scores.

Both options include an easy-to-use online tutorial and program that allows the consumer to see how his credit score would be affected if he changed his financial status. If the consumer pays off a credit card, will the score go up or down? If the consumer buys a new car, how will the credit score be affected?

Information

Is it fair that a company can make money off of grading you and then selling you access to your own personal information? The whole concept drives some consumer activists crazy. Not me. At less than $15 for a report, a score, and valuable information on how to make your score better, it's a bargain.

Debt Collectors

having a debt collector on your case is no fun. If you have the cash and owe the bill, pay it off and be done with it. But if you can't pay or don't owe the money the collector is trying to get from you, the law is on your side.

Insider Secret

When some bill collector is yelling at you for not paying your bills, it is often hard to keep in mind that you are actually in the power position. Remember the business golden rule— those with the gold, rule; since you have the money, you have the power. The person on the other end of the phone doesn't get anything unless you give it to him or her.

A debt collector isn't allowed to call and harass you. First, the calls must generally be made between 8 a.m. and 9 p.m. The collection agency can call you at your workplace, unless you tell it to stop, and then it can't call there again.

When the collection agency contacts you, it has five days to explain how much you owe, to whom you owe it, and how to contest the bill. The collector may not harass or swear at you. The collector is also not allowed to threaten violence or lie to you.

Insider Secret

A new collection practice we are seeing now is old debts taking on a new life. We are hearing from consumers who are telling us that they are being contacted about debts that are 10, 15, and even 20 years old. The debts are being bought for pennies on the dollar, so a $10,000 debt may have been bought by a collection agency for $20. Most states have a statute of limitations for debts. That means you can't be sued after a set period of time, often four years, so despite all the threats there's nothing they can legally do to collect the debt.

If you write the collection agency a letter saying you do not owe the money, the agency must prove that you do before making contact again. If the agency doesn't abide by the law, you have the right to sue it for your actual costs plus $1,000 and attorney's fees.

Before paying a bill to a collection agency, negotiate. Often the agency has paid nearly nothing for your debt, so anything it gets is better than what it currently has, which is nothing. So consider offering a one-time payment that you can afford. An offer of far less than half what is owed is often enough to strike a deal. You'll have to hold your ground, but with collection agencies, a payment in the hand is worth far more than two checks in the mail.

Free Money

One of the best parts of my job is to give out free money. Sometimes I set up a computer out on a sidewalk and have a TV news videographer record the results. Sometimes I give out free money on my radio program. It is easy to do, and I have had the chance to give out hundreds of thousands of dollars.

Now, none of this is my money—in fact, I'm not giving the money away as much as I'm reuniting the cash with its rightful owner. You see, consumers forget they have money sitting in bank accounts. Sometimes a consumer will be part of a class action and won't even know it. So the money is never collected. Occasionally an employer will be sued for not paying proper wages. The employees who are still working at the firm will get their back pay, but employees who have moved on may not know that they have money coming.

In each of those cases the money is put aside in an account where it waits for its rightful owner. And if the owner doesn't claim the cash, it waits for the owner's heirs to pick it up. Its official name is *unclaimed property*. Ask just about any consumer, and she will tell you she knows for sure that she has no money coming. This is why, of course, there are so many millions of dollars waiting to be claimed.

Each state handles unclaimed assets differently. You can call your state capital's information switchboard and ask for the number of the state's unclaimed property division, or you can log on to www.unclaimed.org, the Web site of the National Association of Unclaimed Property Administrators (NAUPA), and find the listings for every state. Contact the state agency by phone or through its Web site to ask that your name be put into the system and a search made for any unclaimed property that should be coming your way.

Advice

A great deal of money goes unclaimed because consumers don't search far and wide. Be sure to check all the states where you have lived or worked. Also check with the states where your employers have been headquartered or where family members have lived or worked.

I often get e-mails from consumers wanting my opinion of a scheme outlined in a piece of mail they've received, in which a company says there is unclaimed cash waiting for pickup if they will split the proceeds with the company. Sometimes the company is asking for only $20 or $30, but other times it demands 10 to 30 percent of the entire amount when the money is turned over to the consumer.

Many consumers figure it is too good to be true, so they throw away the letter. Others figure that part of something is better than all of nothing, so they agree to the terms. Neither is the best move, and here's why.

The company mailing out the letter has simply done a search of the unclaimed property archives and has found money it believes belongs to the person who gets the letter. This is all very legal and happens every day. Still, it's nothing you need to be involved with. Instead, consider the letter a gift—a gift telling you that there is money to be had and you must now find it. Contact your state's unclaimed property division. If the money isn't there, check with other states. It might take you a while, but eventually you will find the cash. Why? Because the company that wrote the letter did, and it doesn't have any records you don't have access to.

I know of only one exception to this. A colleague of mine received a note saying there was money available that belonged to his uncle. He went looking for the money and couldn't find it. He contacted the company that sent him the letter, and it, of course, wouldn't tell him where the money was. Rather than wait for the cash, a sizable amount, to pop up, he struck a deal with the finder for 10 percent. You can do that, too. Remember, if you don't sign up, they don't get any money. If you can't find the money they have found, consider cutting a deal.

Gift Cards and Certificates

gift cards and certificates are one of the hottest topics on my radio show. Someone is always getting ripped off or finding an old certificate and wants to know his or her rights. The recent boom in gift cards has added to the volume of questions. Recently the call screener for my consumer question-and-answer segment on KGO-TV told me half the calls coming in that day had to do with gift certificates. Because of that, we aired a special report to get everyone up-to-date. And since then, there have been many more changes.

Still, money does seem a bit off-putting at times, so there is the gift card, a way to show you care enough to make a guess at the recipient's wants and needs. Gift cards look like credit cards, but that is where the similarity ends. The rules can be confusing, and if you aren't careful, even a high-profile retailer can rip you off.

The first thing you need to know is that a gift card issued by a store never means money in your pocket. The store can give you change back in dollars and cents, but it doesn't have to. It simply must keep track of the credit you have left.

Advice

It is easier to simply give money. When I was a kid, there was no better feeling than seeing one of those oddly shaped money-card envelopes under the Christmas tree. Another great sight was that of a $10 bill fluttering out of a birthday card I had just opened. Money is often a much better option than a gift certificate.

That's why the easiest cards to redeem are those issued by banks and by credit card and financial services companies, like American Express: they can be used just about everywhere. Some even come with PIN numbers allowing the recipient to get money at an ATM.

Most gift certificates, however, are sold through stores, and the individual stores' policies are all over the map. Some say the cards are good forever and will never tack on a service charge; others say the cards expire two years after the date of purchase and come with a per-month maintenance fee of a couple of bucks. Let the card sit for a year, and it could be worthless. The service fee eats away at the card's worth, even though no service has been provided.

For years now, California law prohibited gift certificates from having an expiration date. Now, a new state law places the same rule on gift cards. It also states that no service fees can be attached to the sale of a card. The only loophole in the law is for cards that are all but used up. Cards with less than $5 in value remaining that go unused for two years may be charged a monthly service fee. Other states are considering similar rules.

Retailers are doing so well selling these cards that many are liberalizing their card rules in order to please their customers. About a dozen national chain stores have changed the way they treat gift cards. The stores now say they will reissue lost or stolen cards if the consumer can offer proof of the cards' purchase by showing a sales receipt, credit card statement, or canceled check.

Many Happy Returns

Consumers returning and exchanging gifts are finding themselves more and more at a real disadvantage. Several years ago retailers were liberalizing their return policies as a way to get shoppers in the door. Now those same stores are pulling back, saying consumers must toe the line when it comes to returns.

There are few laws governing return and exchange polices. Under most circumstances, the retailer is free to set any policy it wants as long as the consumer is told before the sale is finalized. Usually that means a sign hanging somewhere near the cash register, but often a written policy on the receipt is good enough to be legal.

This puts the power in the hands of the shopkeeper, but remember that as a consumer you can always vote with your feet. Before making a major purchase, ask about the return and exchange policy. If you don't like what you hear, move on to the next store.

Retailers are allowed to have multiple return policies. You've seen this in action on a sales table, for instance, that has a sign reading, "All sweaters $10—no returns or exchanges." The restocking charges common at electronics stores are another example of multiple policies. Often, some items—for example, big-screen TVs and camcorders—are covered by the fees, while other items—such as stereos and DVD players—are not.

Advice

Here's a rip-off some stores are trying to perpetrate: all returns get pegged at the lowest price for which an item has ever sold at the store. So a sweater you paid $40 for goes on sale for $20 and that's what you receive, even if you have the $40 receipt. If you get caught up in this, complain loudly and consider going to small claims court. I would bet dollars to doughnuts that the judge would rule in your favor.

Restocking fees are really a bribe you pay for the right to return an item. Most restocking fees range between 15 and 25 percent. It is not a good deal. Return a $1,000 TV, and you could be out $250.

I don't like the restocking fees, but it's easy to see where retailers are coming from on this. Many have had real problems with consumers buying an electronics item intending to use it for a party or big event and then returning it—for example, a big-screen TV bought to watch the Super Bowl game and then returned.

So before buying an item, check on the store's restocking-fee policy. That way you won't be forced to pay what is little more than a bribe to return what you don't want or can't use.

Information

You can tell a lot more about a store when making a return or exchange than you can when buying something. If the clerk or shopkeeper is still courteous and helpful even when he or she is giving you money back, that is a store worth shopping in and telling your friends about.

There are a few items that can't be returned, and not just by store policy. Often state law doesn't allow the return of food or plants. Also excluded from returns and exchanges are products for which there are concerns about health and safety, such as swimsuits and underwear. Cars and motorcycles cannot be returned unless a dealership allows it, and that isn't likely unless the vehicle is defective.

Finally, be careful when returning an item with a gift receipt. This is a receipt that lists the item but not the price. Many stores refund the current price of the item, which could be a sale price, when the giver of the gift actually paid full retail. If it's possible, and not too tacky, ask the giver what was paid so that you know what to get for your return.

If you are shopping and see a sign that reads, "No Exchanges, No Returns," believe it. Any shopkeeper willing to post that kind of sign is willing to tell you no when you ask to be the exception.

Privacy

Chapter 3

Telemarketing: Make Them Stop!

There are few things more irritating than getting up from the dinner table to answer the phone, only to find a telemarketer on the line. Your dinner's getting cold while some poor sap is telling you about the joys of taking a new herbal supplement discovered in a rain forest.

Americans have suffered long enough, and now, finally, there are laws on the books to allow you to take control of your home phone. A series of laws culminating in the national do-not-call list now make it possible to silence your phone or punish those who keep calling while pocketing thousands of dollars.

The National Do Not Call Registry has been up and working for more than a year now, and by all indications it is working well. Once a phone number goes on the list, companies are prohibited from calling it for five years. It usually takes about three months after a number is placed on the list before the calls slow down, but after that, consumers experience a drastic reduction in calls. Telemarketers calling numbers on the national registry can be fined $11,000 per phone call.

Information

You can register your phone number
with the National Do Not Call Registry by
either calling 1-888-382-1222 or visiting
the registry's Web site
(www.donotcall.gov).

There are exceptions to the rule. Politicians and political parties can still call you even if your number has been registered. Charities are allowed to keep calling, too. My advice? Think twice before giving money or votes to individuals and organizations that make telemarketing calls.

Here's another loophole, and this is a big one: if you have a business relationship with a company or individual, you can be called. So what's a business relationship? Less than you think. A simple phone call asking the price of an item is probably enough to qualify you for an existing business relationship. Just as with a Hollywood wedding, the fallout from the short-lived relationship often continues long after the relationship has ended. The business has the right to call you for the next 18 months, even if you have registered with the National Do Not Call Registry.

Since an existing business relationship is so important, let me warn you of a scheme that isn't big yet but I predict will be soon. Let's call it the "Do-Not-Call Get-Around Scam." That's when the bad guys try to trick you into saying it's OK for them to call, even if your number is on the Do Not Call Registry. This plays itself out in a number of ways, including through sweepstakes. On the forms for these sweepstakes, somewhere in the small print, consumers will be asked to give their permission to be called even if their numbers are on the do-not-call list.

Insider Secret

Why am I so certain? Because I set up a similar scam several years back for a news report. I put out sweepstakes forms next to a nice-looking Ford Mustang with a sign reading, "Win This Car."

On the sweepstakes form—in the small print—I wrote, "By filling out this form your phone bill will be charged $4.95 a month for nothing." It went on to say the price could go up. Consumer after consumer filled out the form. Had I actually been a bad guy, I would have collected a lot of money.

Warning

Taking the Law into Your Own Hands

by federal law you can sue telemarketers for calling. If you tell a telemarketer not to call and you get another call from that company, you can sue it in small claims court for $500. If the company calls you a third time, the price per call can jump to $1,500.

There are consumers out there making a pretty good second income suing telemarketers who refuse to knock it off. Politicians and charities are excluded, but companies are not, even if you have a so-called existing business relationship. Once you request to be put on the company's internal do-not-call list, the company must stop calling. Consumers filing suit find that companies often settle the cases rather than fight them in court.

Junk Faxes

the best description of junk faxes I've ever heard came from a consumer who said that getting a junk fax is like a home burglary. The person breaks into your house, ties up your phone line, steals a sheet of paper, and then uses your high-priced printer ink to write you a note.

Information

Every fax you receive is estimated to cost 2 cents, so if you receive five advertising faxes a day, at the end of the week you're out 70 cents. By the end of the year, you have spent $36 on advertising you don't want or need. Not a lot of cash, but still it's disheartening to be paying for some company's advertising.

It does feel like a violation, and that's why the law is clear. Unsolicited commercial faxes are illegal. Unless the consumer has given permission, he or she should not be receiving junk faxes.

If you get a junk fax, you can either report it to the Federal Communications Commission, which may or may not take action, or sue the sender. But first you have to figure out where the sender is located, and even though by law that information is supposed to be on the fax, it usually isn't.

Information

To file a Junk Fax Complaint, contact the
Federal Communications Commission
Common Carrier Bureau,
Consumer Information
445 12th Street, S.W.
Washington, D.C. 20554
1-888-CALL-FCC (1-888-225-5322)
A consumer complaint form is also
available at the FCC's Filing a Complaint
Web site (www.fcc.gov/cgb/
complaints.html).

On the bottom of most faxes is a telephone number that offers consumers the chance to *opt out*—that is, to ask not to receive any more faxed messages. Be careful—sometimes those phone numbers backfire and you receive more messages than before. If you respond, the sender now knows you are actually reading the faxes and can be compelled to respond. The thinking goes: if they called this number, maybe they'll call another number and buy something. By responding, you also tell them you have a working fax number.

How to Stop Junk Mail

Unless your first name is "current" and your last name is "resident," you probably feel overwhelmed by junk mail. For most of us, cutting out the AOL and credit card offers alone would go a long way toward making our lives better.

Junk mail is out of control, and the federal government isn't going to make it any better. In fact, the U.S. Postal Service actively encourages junk mailing by giving out addresses and offering special rates to those making mass mailings. Unless you have received explicit sexually oriented material through the mail, your postmaster isn't going to help you. So if you want to cut down on the pile of paper and AOL CDs landing at your house every day, you have to do the work.

You can start by treating your personal information as though it's worth something, because it is. Businesses buy and sell your name every day. Don't give away for free what they are willing to buy. For instance, don't fill out any sweepstakes forms at county fairs. Putting your name and address on one of those forms is like telling the world, "I love junk mail and will do anything for a free offer." This is not the public image you should be trying to cultivate.

Here's what I like to do with junk mail. I treat the prepaid envelopes they send me like my own personal recycling program. I take the credit card offers I receive and stuff them into the prepaid envelopes that come with the magazine subscription offers. Then I take the magazine offers and stuff them into the envelopes for the prepaid credit card offers and put them both in the mail. This is guerrilla consumerism at its finest. Those who make me work must pay. If you decide to do the same thing, be sure you don't accidentally send out personal information.

When sending in product warranty cards, keep the information at a minimum: a name, an address, and the product's serial number. You are trying to make sure you will be notified in case of a recall; you are not trying to help out a company with its marketing efforts. Feel free to use a phony name, and definitely don't write down your annual income or any personal information.

When donating money, tell the charity you do not want your name sold or traded. Remember, if you write your name down, there is a good possibility that someone somewhere is putting it on a list. The range of lists available for sale to marketers is truly stunning. One list I saw offered to sell the names of the participants of a protest march in Washington, D.C. Surely few who signed up realized that their names would be sold in connection with their participation in a march.

After you quit giving out your name, it's time to start taking back your good name. The quickest way to do this is to contact the Direct Marketing Association (DMA). Most legitimate companies making mass mailings are members of the DMA and compare their mailing lists against the DMA's "do not mail" list.

You can register online for $5 at http://dmaconsumers.org or for free by writing to the DMA's Mail Preference Service at P.O. Box 282, Carmel, NY 10512. It takes about three months, but then consumers see a steady decline in mass mailings.

Insider Secret

A good learning experience for your kids is to have them fill out one form using the family pet's name. Then track how that name moves through the world of marketing. It won't be long before your dog or cat starts getting credit card offers, and magazine subscriptions come addressed to the family hamster.

The credit card offers you receive in the mail most often start with your credit report. Each report has a heading, a couple of lines of information that credit card companies buy so that they can send you the offers. You are allowed to opt out of that program by calling 1-888-5-OPT-OUT (1-888-567-8688). One telephone call tells all three major credit bureaus that you no longer want information on preapproved credit card offers.

Along with all those credit card offers, you are probably receiving offers to refinance your home loan. Often the companies sending out the information know where you live and what you owe on your home. How do they know this? The information comes from your county tax assessor's office. The information is a public record and is available to just about anyone who asks. However, two companies are best known for gathering this information, and both offer consumers a way to opt out of their marketing services:

Acxiom (1-877-774-2094)

Dataquick (1-877-970-9171)

Your property information will still be collected and sold, but it will not be placed on a marketing list.

Finally, when you receive the yearly privacy statements from your bank, credit card issuers, and other financial service companies, read them carefully and take any opportunity to opt out of the sharing of your personal information.

Information?

You might also want to directly contact several of the companies and organizations that send you the most junk mail. Here is a list of the bigger nationwide firms:

America Online (1-888-265-8003)

Publishers Clearing House (1-800-645-9242)

ADVO (1-860-285-6100)

Valpak (1-800-676-6878)

Have you ever noticed that when you buy one item out of a catalog, you get about a dozen similar catalogs through the mail over the next few weeks? That's because there is a company called Abacus that keeps track of consumers who buy from catalogs. It puts together mailing lists that are sold to catalog companies. If you don't want to receive a dozen catalogs every time you place an order, opt out of the Abacus list by calling the company at 1-800-518-4453.

Getting an unlisted phone number can dramatically reduce the number of mail offers you receive. Some phone companies charge for this service, usually 50 cents a month. I know that's not much money, but there's no reason for you to pay *not to have something.* So instead, have the listing put in your dog's name or maybe your mom's maiden name. You are allowed to do that, and it's free.

Information

One of the true heroes of privacy protection is Beth Givens. She is the founder and director of the Privacy Rights Clearinghouse. More than a decade ago she was working to protect our privacy. It was a lonely job back then, with few understanding the ground we were losing in the fight for privacy. Beth had the vision and the stick-to-itiveness to fight identity theft and the blasé attitude that made it possible. Many of the privacy laws we take for granted and issues we discuss daily go back to Beth's early warnings and legislative fights. The Privacy Rights Clearinghouse (www.privacyrights.org) is still on the cutting edge, advising consumers and lawmakers of the perils of lost privacy and how to deal with the problem.

How to Stop Spam

he fight against junk e-mail—spam—is finally under way; however, it is off to a very slow start. A new federal law that was pitched as drawing a line in the sand is really just a starting point. Called the CAN-SPAM Act, the law has four main provisions:

- The subject line must be truthful. A subject line that reads "A note from work" on an email that is actually an advertisement for a trip to Florida is now illegal. The true sender of the e-mail must also be noted.

- Using someone else's Internet address to send spam is now illegal, as is hacking into another person's computer to send e-mail.

- All spam must now come with a legitimate opt-out e-mail address so that consumers can tell the company to stop sending the e-mail.

- The company that's selling the product, not just the company hired to send the e-mail, is held responsible for breaking the law.

Breaking this law can lead to multimillion-dollar fines and jail time of up to five years. It's doubtful that many spammers will do time, but the fear is now out there, and that is a good thing. Casual spammers will look for other opportunities.

Information

Here is a business opportunity for someone in the computer field: Set up a service that notifies businesses to stop sending e-mail to a particular consumer. Set up a database of corporations doing business in the United States, and send out a note to each one that reads, "Do not spam John Q. Public at [insert e-mail address here]."

Many Internet service providers offer spam filters, and other filters are available for about thirty bucks at computer stores and on the Internet. *PC World* magazine does a great job of keeping track of this type of software; check out its latest advice at www.pcworld.com.

Spam pornography is becoming a big problem; even products that are not specifically explicit are now being marketed with suggestive messages and pictures. Congress has directed the Federal Trade Commission (www.ftc.gov) to work on this problem. If you have any suggestions, let the FTC know.

Most anti-spam activists in the United States are disappointed with this new law because it doesn't go far enough. The activists wanted the opt-in system rather than this opt-out version. There's no telling how this will shake out; after trying the opt-out system for a while, Americans may be pleased with the results, or there could be a change to the more restrictive United Kingdom system. In the U.K. spam is simply illegal. A company must get a consumer's permission before e-mailing an advertisement.

Little Brother

Y ou are being spied on and watched. That's not even debated anymore. There are dozens of agencies and thousands of individuals who make money keeping track of your personal life. It may sound very Orwellian—Big Brother is watching, and all—but Beth Givens, the director of the Privacy Rights Clearinghouse, says that Big Brother isn't nearly as much of a problem as the dozens of Little Brothers who are peeking into your life. What used to be called *gossip* is now called *information* and is compiled, sold, and traded all without your knowledge.

There are, of course, the three major credit reporting companies: Equifax, Experian, and TransUnion. These are the companies that keep track of your credit and bill paying. If you take out a loan, these companies will be told. If you miss a payment, they will be told. They, in turn, compile this information and sell it to other companies that want to know more about you.

There are laws about who can see what and when, but generally you have to give permission to a company before it can see your personal dossier.

Warning

If you think your medical condition is just between you and your doctor, you haven't been reading the fine print on the forms you have been filling out. Much of your medical history is being compiled by the Medical Information Bureau (www.mib.com). A new federal law makes it possible for any consumer to see, and correct, the information in his or her personal MIB report. The cost is $9, unless you've been turned down for insurance because of MIB information; then the report is available at no charge.

Have you filed an insurance claim? If so, you have a C.L.U.E., which is a report with an agency called the Comprehensive Loss Underwriting Exchange. If you file a claim on your home, there will be two entries: one for you and one for your home. Get enough dings on your report, and neither you nor your home will be insurable at a decent price.

In the past, just asking your insurance agent a question about a claim could result in a ding, but now state laws and C.L.U.E. policy are changing, so that a question does not count against your score. To buy a C.L.U.E. report about you or your property, visit the ChoiceTrust Web site (www .choicetrust.com).

Insider Secret

I once reported on a famous case in which a shopper slipped and fell in a grocery store. He filed a claim, and there was no argument that the fall was real. It seemed like an open-and-shut case until the supermarket's attorney challenged the shopper, saying that a check of the shopper's loyalty card showed that he had bought a fair amount of alcoholic beverages. The shopper's attorney was stunned and angry, and the store settled rather than go further trying to use that information. I know of no other lawsuits in which the loyalty card–tracking mechanism has been brought up; however, keep in mind that it has happened.

Supermarket chains are to be commended for how carefully they guard the information they can access through their loyalty card programs. Most stores tell us they don't keep track of individual shoppers. Privacy advocates are concerned, though, that if the wrong people got hold of this information, a file could be built tracking the liquor, sugar cookies and other less healthful items a consumer purchases.

There is no denying the cost savings many shoppers find with loyalty cards, but when signing up for one of these programs make sure you select a trustworthy store.

Identity Theft

dentity theft has become a growth business. The stakes are high, and the chances of the thief's getting caught are low. The crime is so widespread now that even consumers who are extremely careful can be ripped off. If your identity is stolen and used, you will spend countless hours and potentially several hundred dollars dealing with the issue.

If you get caught up in an identity theft scheme, notify one of the three major credit reporting agencies: Experian, Equifax, or TransUnion. By law, if you notify one, it must notify the others.

Ask for a fraud alert to be added to your report. An alert warns lenders that you may not actually be you. This means that instant loans, such as at a furniture store, will in all likelihood not be granted. The alerts stay on your report for 90–180 days, so keep that in mind; you may want to request an extension.

Next, notify the local police. This is important because you will need to prove that you are a victim, not a deadbeat. You will need a copy of the police report, so ask for one when making the initial contact. If you have problems with credit reporting agencies or lenders, a copy of the report will end a lot of the hassle. If you have a police report, you have the upper hand, since the lenders can't keep accusing you of taking out the loan or not paying the bill.

Information

My identity was stolen, but I lucked out. The police busted the ring that stole my identity before my information was used. Still, my situation shows how these things work. My information was put together with the information of other Michael Finneys. There was me the consumer advocate, there was Michael Finney the police officer, and there was the high-tech-business owner named Michael Finney. Our personal private information had been woven together into this conglomerate. Since we all live in the same area, the information would have in all likelihood worked for the thieves. The three Michael Finneys would have been on the hook and spending countless hours trying to straighten out the mess.

Notify your bank, current lenders, and credit card companies as well. That way, if unusual activity is spotted, those financial institutions may be able to stop a problem before it gets out of hand.

If you believe your driver's license is involved, contact your state motor vehicles agency. Most states drag their feet, but some will issue a new driver's license number if the consumer has a good reason and makes a stink.

Advice

Buy a paper shredder. They cost less than $40 now and make a real difference in protecting your privacy. Ask anyone who has ever been divorced, and you'll be told that a shredder is a very good idea. Get a crosscut shredder—they turn paper into confetti and are now as cheap as strip shredders. At the very least you should shred all your monthly bank, credit card, and brokerage account statements. Also shred old bills, paycheck stubs, and any mail you received that includes personal information beyond your name and address.

Most consumers spend too much time worrying about their private information on the Internet and not enough time concerned with their information in the physical world. We often see identity theft cases that start when a store or restaurant employee steals the card numbers of customers, using a device that can read the magnetic stripe on the back of a credit card. This crime is called *skimming*, and as credit card readers get smaller and more portable, the problem is getting worse.

Privacy 69

Warning

Have you heard of *dumpster diving?* It's one way that thieves get personal private information. They go through the garbage cans outside of businesses. I have made several dumpster diving trips myself while putting together TV news reports. I have found bank account numbers, driving records, and medical records, as well as accounts of stock brokerage trades where investors' net worth was listed along with their names and addresses. Workplaces tend to do a good job watching out for their own privacy and a not-so-good job watching out for the privacy of their clients and customers.

Insurance

Chapter 4

Why You Should Dump Your Insurance Agent/

Why You Should Get an Insurance Agent

not long ago, if you wanted insurance, you had to have an insurance agent. Insurance agents wrote insurance policies, and there was no way around having an agent. This, even though agents were represented in popular culture as pushy salesmen who, once inside your home, refused to leave. That image was overdone and, like any stereotype, unfair to the vast majority of those being stereotyped. Nonetheless, the image remains, and to this day many consumers will do whatever it takes to avoid dealing with an insurance agent.

If that's you, the Internet can be your insurance-shopping friend. Web sites sell, or at least start the selling process, online rather than in your living room or at the agent's office. You do not have to like the person, because there is no person.

Online insurance services make it easy to compare what the insurance companies are offering. However, when looking at these sites, remember that the insurance companies use the Internet as a sales tool, so don't look for full disclosure. Consumers often get suckered into a Web site by a headline that reads something like, "Low rates guaranteed! One hundred thousand dollars of life insurance for just ten dollars a month!" The headline is true: that policy is actually available—just not to you.

When drawing up their ads, insurance companies and Web sites representing insurance companies always assume the best, so the $10-a-month quote is for a 25-year-old female who has never smoked and is in perfect health.

Warning

How did you pick your insurance company? If you are like most of us, it's the one your parents used. Young people don't know how to buy insurance, so they just go to the company their parents used. The problem with that is, when *their* parents were young, *they* didn't know how to buy insurance so they just went with the company *their* parents used. Many families are now three or four generations into an insurance company, and no one has ever comparison-shopped for price and service.

Once you go deeper into the application process, you'll find that the rate quote you can actually get will, as the ads announce in the small print, "vary substantially" from the example first given. The come-on quote has so little to do with your situation that it is nonsense. Fill out the online application with your real age and health profile, and you'll get a much higher quote. Still, if you put in accurate information, the prices that the sites eventually give you are pretty close to what you'll be charged for a policy.

So, why do you need an insurance agent if all this is available online? You don't need an agent, especially if you are that mythical 25-year-old woman looking only for life insurance. The online rates are so low, and you are so perfect a client, that insurance companies will be falling all over themselves to get your business. However, if you are 55 and have high blood pressure, an agent can be crucial. He or she should be talking with the insurance company and making the case for insuring you at a reasonable rate. It works that way for car, homeowners, and other insurance policies, too.

If you have an agent, you have a professional on your team—someone to advise you on what you need and to act as a buffer between you and the insurance company. A good insurance agent is your personal insurance adviser, a professional dedicated to saving you money and protecting you from grief.

If the agent I just described doesn't sound like your agent, there's a problem, and you might want to fire him or her. If the first time you hear of a major increase in your premium is when the bill arrives from the company, you should start thinking about firing your agent. The agent should be keeping track of these things and talking to you about them. If your agent has never called you with an idea to save money or has never stepped in and worked to get you a better deal, it's time to fire that agent.

Feel free to use the word *fired,* and say that I am the one who put you up to it. There are far too many insurance agents out there who mistakenly believe they work for the insurance companies and not for their clients. If that is your agent, fire him or her and buy your insurance on the Internet, or find another agent.

If you are looking for an independent agent, I suggest you start by looking at large firms that have been doing business in their area for decades. Those firms often have considerable clout in the marketplace. In most areas there are one or two respected firms. Once you find their names, start asking around about the individual agents who work there. An established agent is often more savvy, while a newer agent will work harder to get your business.

If you are looking to go with a particular name-brand insurance company that has a staff of agents, you want to look for the standouts. In most areas there are one or two agents with each big company who are the most respected in the community. Track down those people and you'll be happy with your service.

How to Buy Life Insurance

You do not need life insurance if you don't have a family or other loved ones who depend upon you for support. If that's you, you are excused from this chapter. Many young couples are told that they should buy insurance now because it will cost more later on. That's true, but it's true for everything. If you don't buy a car now, it will cost more later on. That argument is not a good reason for buying a car, and it's not by itself a good reason for buying life insurance either. Every dime spent on insurance premiums is a dime not available for investments.

Family wage earners who have responsibilities now have responsibilities after they pass on. Families that are left destitute often end up that way because the family moneymaker didn't want to think about his or her own death or what would happen after he or she died. Don't leave your family in a bad situation because you didn't want to deal with the inevitable. Quit avoiding the subject and buy life insurance.

Here's the big question: how much life insurance do you need? The rule of thumb used to be that a wage earner needed to buy life insurance in the amount of four times his or her annual pay. A person making $50,000 a year would be looking at a $200,000 policy. Some in the insurance industry would have you believe that four times your salary isn't nearly enough. Often, eight times the annual salary is cited. So which is it? Neither.

Advice

If you are planning to become a parent, or another life-changing event is about to happen, feel free to look ahead, but remember that you could end up paying for a policy you don't now need and may never need. It all boils down to your tolerance for risk. If you have a high tolerance, you should consider putting off the purchase of life insurance until you need it that very day—for instance, buying life insurance when you or your spouse is confirmed as pregnant, rather than when you decide to have a baby. Consumers who want to limit risk should look at buying a policy sooner rather than later.

A simple formula that doesn't take into account the age of your kids and your spouse's earnings just isn't very helpful. Add in the cost of educating the kids and the mortgage payment, and now you are getting closer to figuring out how much insurance is needed.

In the best of all worlds, your family would be completely taken care of forever, but since you are looking at the possibility of your own death, the "best of all worlds" scenario is already a goner. Forget perfect and instead look at what's doable, now and later.

Advice

Your death should not be like winning the lottery for your heirs, nor should it be a quick trip to poverty. It's a balancing act between meeting your current needs and taking care of business after you leave the stage. The only thing sadder than a family left destitute after the death of a loved one is seeing a family left rich by a person who never had much disposable income because of large insurance premiums.

If your spouse makes more money than you, take that into consideration. If you live near family and those left behind will have help taking care of the kids, take that into consideration, too. Before figuring out exactly what you think you need, remember that insurance is only for what you can't afford to do without. If you die, your spouse doesn't need a new car or a vacation. She needs time to get her life together and enough money to carry on without a major shift in her lifestyle, either up or down.

Finally, don't decide how much you need until you know the cost. When walking into a restaurant, many customers plan to order the biggest steak, but once they find the price on the menu, they often order the "petite" cut. When shopping for insurance, need and price must both be weighed.

Shop around for the best price; there can be huge differences. There is no evil here, just insurance companies doing their best to weigh their risks. Many insurance companies will notice that they are selling too many policies to one kind of client—say, healthy young men—while selling too few policies to another kind—for example, middle-aged women in average health. To balance its risk, an insurance company may decide to raise the rates for young men and drop the rates for middle-aged women until the correct balance is found.

Another reason for varying rates is that insurance companies often specialize in one type of client, such as teachers or those with large families. If you fit their criteria, the deals can be unbeatable; if you don't make their cut, the rates can be extremely high.

Which Life Insurance Should You Buy?

Term insurance

If you want to keep things simple and straightforward, you will buy term life insurance. That's where you pay an annual premium. And if you die, the insurance company makes a payout.

Information

With life insurance, you are betting that you are going to die, and the insurance company is betting that you are going to live. The lower your premium, the lower your chance of dying. The higher the premium, the better your chance of dying. Compare your premiums with those of friends and relatives, and you might get a nice surprise.

Term insurance is called *term* because it is offered for a set period of time, or term. The policies renew each year, for the same payout amount you first bought. The premium goes up every year because every year you get older and closer to death.

Most policies are now sold with set premiums for a certain period of time; these are called *level term* policies. Most companies offer a single nonincreasing rate for 10, 20, or 30 years. The longer the level term, the higher the premium, because the insurance company is taking on a higher risk in the later years.

Insider Secret

A common saying is, "Life insurance is sold, not bought." That is, few consumers wake up saying, "I must have life insurance." Instead, an insurance agent calls and tells the consumer, "You must have life insurance." Because of that dynamic, consumers waste a huge amount of money overpaying for insurance. I've seen estimates that as much as 10 percent of the nearly $100 billion spent per year on life insurance is squandered. So don't be "sold" life insurance; go shopping for it just as you would any other big-ticket item, such as a car or stereo.

A 35-year-old male in good physical health can buy a $500,000 10-year level term policy for $190 annually. If that same 35-year-old male wants a 20-year level policy, that same $500,000 coverage will cost $300. If he wants a 30-year fixed premium, the annual cost goes up to $600.

Because premiums increase dramatically as more time is added to a level term policy, many consumers opt for the 10-

year term. The premiums are good, but if insurance is still needed after the 10 years are up, the policyholder is looking at a huge increase. The 35-year-old male in good physical health we talked about above pays only $190 a year for his $500,000 during the first 10 years, but at 45 the $500,000 policy increases to $405.

Do the math and you'll find that the 20-year level term premiums would run our consumers $6,000 over the 20-year life of the policy, while the 10-year policy with an additional renewed 10 years would run $5,950. That looks like a $50 savings, but remember that there was a lot of risk for that half a C-note. If the consumers had become sick and not died, the insurance company may have declined to issue a new policy, or charged substantially more.

Advice

Some insurance agents can play fast and loose with the truth when explaining how the investments will pan out. A bit like politicians projecting nothing but good times ahead, some agents see nothing but a rosy future when predicting the return on your insurance investment. Keep that in mind when looking at charts and graphs of how your money will grow.

Cash-value insurance

These insurance policies are complicated and combine life insurance with investments. Flying under a variety of names like *whole life, universal life, variable life,* and *universal variable life,* these policies insure your life and work as an investment. With most of these policies—although there are exceptions—the death benefit amount is guaranteed. So if the policy is issued as a $100,000 policy, your beneficiary receives the full $100,000 if you die. The exception is found in the policies allowing the policyholder to select the investments. Since money can be lost, the death benefit can drop below the listed dollar amount.

Advice

When buying term insurance, consider buying two or more policies rather than one giant policy. If you buy more than one, you can stagger their expiration dates so that they expire when you no longer need them. If you have two children, one 12 years old and the other 7 years old, you can buy two separate policies: one that expires in 10 years so that the older child's education is covered, and a 15-year level term policy for the 7 year old. That way, you can ensure in the event of your death that there is college money for both of the kids without spending more than necessary. You may buy as many policies as you want, so staggering several policies is often the most cost-effective.

The investment component—and it is nearly always called a *component*—can be in stocks or bonds. Either the insurance company or the policyholder can control the investment. The earnings will be tax deferred—that is, no taxes are paid until the money is taken out of the account. There is even a way to avoid those payments, and that is to borrow against the cash value of the policy. Since it's your money guaranteeing the loan, interest rates are often extremely low, and there may not be a repayment schedule, meaning that the policyholder can keep the loan going indefinitely.

Many cash-value policies offer a minimum return, but in today's financial environment the guarantee isn't anything to write home about.

If you are confused, that just means you are paying attention. These cash-value policies are complicated and best suited to investors who are willing to learn and read about them. Consumers often use these policies as forced savings accounts. That's probably better than not saving at all, but alone it is not a good enough reason to become involved in such a complex investment and insurance situation.

The question you must answer before buying a cash-value policy is this: Why do you want to combine your insurance and investments into one vehicle? If you don't know why, you shouldn't buy a cash-value policy.

Five Insurance Policies You Don't Need and Two that Might Be Worth the Money

The policies to avoid

Insurance is a good, profitable business to be involved with, and here's your proof: there is some company out there willing to insure just about anything, from car payments to weddings. Most of these *add-on* policies should be avoided.

Cancer insurance. This insurance kicks in if you get cancer or sometimes only if you die of cancer. Any other infirmity or disease, and you are on your own. We are all scared of the big C, and these policies play to that fear. Still, your insurance dollar would be better spent on standard life and health insurance policies. Some forms of this insurance are so costly that some state insurance commissioners have banned cancer insurance altogether.

Credit card insurance #1. Let's say you lose your job or get sick and can't work. This insurance kicks in and pays your monthly credit card bill. Or at least that's what you are led to believe. What really happens is that the credit card company freezes your credit card bill. No payments are expected, and interest charges are stopped, but the bill doesn't actually get paid down.

This insurance is usually too costly, and most consumers should avoid it. There is an exception: if you know a layoff is coming in your workplace, this insurance can be worth it, but make sure you read and understand the fine print.

Credit card insurance #2. This insurance kicks in if your card is lost or stolen. It offers to pay any illegally made charges. Sold for as much as $79 a year, this is the ultimate in unneeded insurance. Most credit card companies waive all charges if the consumer lets the company know the card is missing, and by law the consumer is only on the hook for the first $50 anyway.

Credit life insurance. This pays off a specific debt if you die. Often, mortgage companies and car dealerships sell credit life insurance. At first it can sound like a good deal for your family, but the insurance is usually overpriced and seldom used. Most insurance policies pay about 70 percent of their premiums back to consumers, while credit life pays as little as 40 percent back.

One of the biggest problems with credit life insurance is that consumers don't shop around. Premiums for a policy that protects a $20,000 car are so high that they can often buy a $100,000 term life insurance policy. Don't buy anything if you don't know what it's worth—especially an insurance policy.

Flight insurance. It's still out there, but the machines in the airports aren't as obvious as they were in years past. For a few bucks you can insure your life if there's a plane crash. This is not a good deal because plane crashes don't happen much, and when they do, the airlines often give the victims' families huge cash settlements.

The two policies that should be considered

Lift ticket insurance. Since last year, ski resorts have been able to sell insurance to those who buy season lift tickets. The passes are good for a ski season and cost anywhere from $300 to $1,300 and more. With lift ticket insurance, if the skier is kept off the slope because of injury or illness, the cash value of the unused portion of the lift ticket is rebated. This insurance is best for students who can't afford to lose the price of a lift ticket.

Wedding insurance. This insurance kicks in if there is trouble on the big day. It reimburses the couple if the wedding must be canceled due to bad weather, because a caterer or other major player goes out of business, or because the bride or groom or a close relative gets sick or injured. This insurance does not pay if the wedding is canceled because of cold feet.

Advice

The most important thing to know about insurance is that you should never buy it for a loss you can afford to absorb on your own. Insurance is for the unexpected extremely expensive times in life when you need a hefty amount of cash to put yourself back together. That's why theater ticket insurance, which is becoming a big seller, isn't worth the ten bucks often charged. If anything, missing a night of theater could save you money, since you won't be going out to eat and paying for cabs or parking.

Disability Insurance

You are far more likely to be hurt and unable to work than you are to die prematurely. The latest statistic I've seen shows that a 35-year-old worker is six times more likely to be disabled than to die. That is the reasoning behind disability insurance. Strangely, most adults don't carry it.

Many think Social Security will kick in and they'll be fine, but Social Security disability is hard to qualify for and pays less than $1,500 a month. To be truly protected, you must buy your own disability insurance policy.

There are two types of disability insurance: *short term,* which lasts from two weeks to two years and is often part of a benefits package that workers receive from their employers; and *long term,* which lasts up to five years or to the age of 65, depending on the policy.

Most workplaces don't provide long-term disability insurance as part of the standard benefits package but do offer group policies as an add-on. For a few dollars a week, employees can buy disability insurance. The problem with work-related policies is that if you leave the job, you leave your coverage behind, and because of age or medical conditions, you may not be able to buy your own disability coverage. Still, if you don't see a change in your employment status or in your health, a company-supplied policy may be enough—again, it all comes down to your tolerance for risk.

Warning

It is extremely important that you know exactly what your policy defines as disabled. Some policies include disfigurement as a disability, which is important for a salesperson. Other policies do not consider scars and such a disability, and that may be fine for a worker who has limited contact with the public.

Before buying insurance, let me give you the good news: disability insurance payments are not taxable. That means you don't need to buy enough to cover your whole salary, just your take-home pay. Many companies allow workers to buy coverage up to 60 percent of their pretaxed paycheck, and that is a good guide for those buying individual policies as well.

To save money on your policy, buy one that kicks in six months after you are injured. There are policies that start after three months and even after one month, but the premiums can be nearly double since a worker is much more likely to use one of those policies.

Next you need to consider when the policy will end. There is coverage—and it's pretty cheap—that offers benefits for as little as two years. A more common policy provision makes payments for five years, and then you are on your own. Don't buy either of these two policies; you need coverage that will take you up to a retirement age of 65 years. While you're at it, consider paying a bit more and adding a cost-of-living adjustment to your policy. With that adjustment, every year your disability payment goes up, similarly to how your salary would have increased.

Insider Secret

Some disability policies give full benefits to a worker who can no longer do his or her old job. For instance, a TV anchor who injures his back and can't sit for long periods of time would be considered completely disabled. Other disability policies aren't so generous in their definition and only pay when the worker can't perform any job.

If you buy an individual policy rather than going through your company, you'll pay about ten times as much for the same coverage. And since it is an individual policy, you'll need to get a medical examination and go through a good deal of paperwork. Most disability insurance companies will allow you to buy coverage for up to 80 percent of your current income, but again, 60 percent is plenty for most.

Disability coverage has its own lingo, and the most important phrases are these two: *noncancelable* and *guaranteed renewable*. With noncancelable coverage, the insurance company can never increase your premium or drop the coverage. With guaranteed renewable coverage, you can't be dropped but your premium can go up. It is slightly better than it sounds at first, because the insurer cannot raise your rate alone; instead, it can only raise the rates of everyone in your coverage group.

Advice

Most policies don't require the insured to keep paying the premium if she is disabled. Still, to be on the safe side, get a written confirmation of that before stopping the payments. You wouldn't want to lose your coverage just as you need it because some insurance company found a loophole.

If you are partially disabled and can work part time or can do a different but lower-paying job, the insurance company will work out a deal allowing you to be employed without taking home less pay than the complete disability payment. Some policies will pay a partial payment if you are disabled but can still work at your current job. You most often see the partial payments when the insured loses the use of his arms or legs or when eyesight is lost.

Seven Ways to Save Money on Health Insurance

a s I'm writing this, our American health care system is in crisis. Consumers and their employers are paying too much, the working poor have no coverage at all, and the frustration level is continuing to rise. The disconnect between Washington and the public is so complete that the Food and Drug Administration is threatening the elderly with steep fines and jail time if they continue to go to Canada and buy the lower-cost drugs available there.

Every day complaints come in to my hotline about insurance companies that refuse to pay for treatments that are clearly covered and HMOs that are shoddily run.

Since most of us get our medical coverage through our employers, our choices are limited. We can change insurance companies if our employers offer open enrollment, but even then the choice is often between bad and worse. So the best defense against shoddy medical care is a good offense.

Study your plan. Most consumers have no idea of the rules and regulations surrounding their health plans. That leads to many of the problems that land in my lap. Consumers don't yet seem to understand that few companies are willing to bend the rules anymore. All too often we see companies looking for ways to avoid paying a bill. If the consumer gives them a chance not to pay, that's what some of the worst offenders will do. So know your plan and go by the rules. It may not be right, but it is the way things work.

Don't go where you aren't wanted. Many hospitals may not be part of your plan, so don't show up at an out-of-plan hospital unless you are willing to pay for the visit out-of-pocket. There are times when you can argue that you had no choice, but it's easier to go to an "in-plan provider" than to argue about why you went to the "outside vendor."

Negotiate. If something isn't covered, or the co-payment is high, try to get the doctor, clinic, or hospital to drop the amount *you* have to pay. Try to keep things on a very personal basis if you are in a small office. If you make a fantastic apple pie, offer that up. If you are a painter and can see that the office needs a fresh coat of paint, offer to do the job. Look for ways to make the doctor more comfortable, and you'll work out some off-the-books deals.

Open a health care spending account. I am constantly amazed at how many employees where I work don't take advantage of the company's health care spending accounts. There are different versions, but here's what they have in common: They allow workers to put aside money that is not taxed. A special medical account is set up, and the money placed there can be used for medical purposes such as co-payments and prescriptions. Since the money is not taxed, for the average worker it's like getting a 25 percent discount on all medical purchases. The catch is that you lose what you didn't spend at the end of the year. So deciding how much money to put in an account is critical.

Coordinate plans. If you and your spouse both work and have an insurance plan, make sure that you get every dime coming to you. You'll have twice the headaches and twice the paperwork, but with some planning you can substantially cut your health care bills.

Advice

If your company does not have a medical savings account, ask it to set one up. It's amazing how many employers don't offer these plans simply because no one has ever asked for them.

Don't get bitten by the COBRA. Just about everyone knows the basics of the COBRA law. If you lose your job, under most circumstances the company must allow you to stay on its group medical plan for up to three years. The downside is that you must pay the premiums. A family premium can easily top $500 a month. I have talked with plenty of workers who found better deals on their own buying an individual plan.

There is power in numbers. If you have to buy your own coverage, look first to groups where you are a member—fraternal groups and professional organizations, for instance. Many organizations offer group health plans. eBay offers group coverage to its Power Sellers; if the policy works for you, get out your old stuff and auction it off to pay for your medical coverage.

Homeowners' and Renters' Insurance

buying a homeowners' policy is a no-brainer. That's because if you don't buy a policy, the mortgage holder will buy one for you and send you the bill. The policy is expensive and only covers the lender's losses, not yours. If you own your home outright and don't have a mortgage, you need a policy because you have too much to lose in the event of a disaster.

Homeowners' policies are standardized across the country and from one company to another. Prices vary, and add-on niceties can differ, but for the most part insurance companies offer policies that range from the very basic to the nearly all-inclusive. None of the policies include flood or earthquake coverage, so if you need either one of those, you must buy it separately. They aren't cheap, though, and can double your insurance bill.

Here's what a basic homeowners' policy covers: the house itself, including most pools, fences, and outbuildings. It also covers the items in your home: furniture, clothing, and personal belongings. Your living expenses, if the house becomes uninhabitable because of a disaster or fire, are also usually covered. Your homeowners' policy offers liability coverage as well. If your dog bites your neighbor's child, the insurance company will pay the medical bills and provide an attorney to fight any court actions.

Advice

Should you buy earthquake or flood insurance? Those are big questions these days. The answer depends on how much of your home you own. If you own the place free and clear, it's definitely worth considering, but if you just bought the house and put down, say, 3 percent, you don't have enough money on the line to bother with those high-deductible policies. As your investment and ownership of the home grows, you'll need to reevaluate your position.

How much you are paid for a property loss is determined when the policy is bought. If you pick an actual-cash-value policy, you'll get paid what something is worth on the open market. If your three-year-old big-screen TV gets stolen, you're looking at getting about a third of what you paid.

If you selected a policy that pays replacement value, you'll get a settlement that pays enough for you to buy a brand-new TV to replace the stolen one.

There are several levels of payment for the actual structure as well. Some policies will only pay the dollar amount listed on the policy; others will pay whatever it takes to rebuild. However, even with replacement-cost policies there are limits to the insurance company's generosity. Some policies take a middle ground between those two extremes. There are sound reasons to buy any of the policies; what's important is that you make an informed decision.

Renters' insurance is similar to a homeowners' policy, but the rental unit is not insured the same way a home is covered. Renters' insurance protects the policyholder's clothing and household belongings just like a homeowners' policy, but the building itself is only covered under special circumstances. Most renters don't know this, but if they cause damage to their building, even if it's accidental, they can be held liable.

So if you are cooking and there is a kitchen fire, your landlord can bill you for the damage. It's *fire legal liability*. A good renters' policy protects you against that kind of loss. If you are a college student, you probably don't need the coverage. If you are a working adult, you probably do.

Condominium insurance takes in parts of both homeowners' and renters' policies. These policies usually don't cover the outside structure but do insure improvements made to the inside of the unit.

Ten Easy Ways to Drop Your Homeowners' Premium

1. Up your deductible. Many homeowners are still carrying a $100 or $500 deductible, which is expensive coverage. Move your deductible up to $2,000, and you can save up to 40 percent on your premium. It's not as though you are losing much coverage, since smaller claims can get your policy canceled, so most consumers don't submit them anyway.

2. Don't get a big dog or a wooden shake roof. Both are potential trouble just waiting to happen. Dogs bite and wood burns; enough said.

3. Buy a home security system. Smoke alarms and a monitored burglar alarm can drop your rates another 10 percent and offer real safety to your family.

4. Have good credit. Insurance companies have found that consumers with bad credit file more claims, so the lower your credit score, the higher your insurance bill.

5. Lump your homeowners' insurance in with your car insurance. Many companies offer a steep discount, another 10 percent, to those who bundle their policies together.

6. Don't file claims. The industry keeps track of people who file claims and properties that are claim-prone. If you are one or live in one, you'll pay more.

7. Don't put in a pool or set up a trampoline. Those two items have a nickname in the world of insurance and law—"attractive nuisance." That means kids are more likely to jump over your fence to get to them, and hurt themselves in the process. Nuisances, attractive or not, come with a price.

8. Retire. Many companies figure that if you are retired, you are in your home more; and that means if there is a problem, say a fire, you'll spot it sooner and there will be less damage.

9. Look for a group policy. Some companies offer group insurance to employees of certain companies or to those in specific professions, like teaching.

10. Stick with the same company year after year. The company knows it's cheaper to retain a customer than it is to go looking for a new one, so many offer their long-term customers a 15 percent discount.

Win a Fight with Your Homeowners' Insurance Carrier

back 10 or 12 years ago, insurance companies looked at a house fire as a marketing opportunity. The company adjuster would arrive with a spiffy clean helmet, look around the property, and start writing checks. It was a good, very public way to prove that the company took care of its policyholders.

Those days are gone forever. Now the adjuster arrives and starts looking at the property and the small print on the contract. In most cases, the adjuster is not trying to rip off the consumer, but he isn't there to make friends either. Now it is simply a business relationship, and it often even feels like an adversarial one at that.

So what happens if the settlement offer is not as much as you believe it should be? Start by making your case to the insurance adjuster, and if that fails, talk to your agent. Explain to the agent that you expect her to fight for your rights. A good agent will jump into the fray and try to set things right. If the agent fails to get you an acceptable settlement or fails to even try, you might want to hire a *public adjuster*.

Public adjusters are just like insurance adjusters, except—and this is a big exception—they work for the public and not for an insurance company. After a major fire or hurricane you see these people out in force looking over damage with the same hawklike eyes as the insurance company adjusters.

These professionals are just as qualified as any insurance adjuster, but they work for you. They are interested in getting you a fair settlement, rather than containing the insurance company's costs.

A public adjuster appraises the damage and then files claims and reports. If there is a gap between what the insurance company offers and what the public adjuster thinks is needed, the battle goes into high gear with negotiations and new appraisals and estimates. A good public adjuster is a bit like a lawyer fighting for your rights and looking to cut a deal.

Information ?

Many public adjusters are listed with the National Association of Public Insurance Adjusters (www.napia.com) and are in the yellow pages. A good insurance agent should also know the names of the respected public insurance adjusters in your area.

So what's the downside? A public adjuster is not cheap. So before hiring one, exhaust other possibilities and then get in writing just what you will be paying for the services. Often the fee is a percentage of the final settlement. Ten or 15 percent is not considered out of line, depending on what the state insurance commissioner has approved and the work that has just been carried out.

With that kind of money being spent, don't hire an adjuster without first getting recommendations, and check him out with your state insurance commissioner and Better Business Bureau.

If this all sounds like a big hassle and a lot of work, that's because it is, but with so much money—and your family's home—on the line, you just have to find it within yourself to do all the hard work that will get you back to normal again.

Auto Insurance

auto insurance is really six different insurance issues all rolled into one policy. *Collision* covers the cost of fixing your car if you get in a wreck. *Property liability* pays for the damage you do to the other driver's car during a wreck. *Personal injury protection* pays the medical expenses for you and your passengers, while *bodily injury liability* pays for the other party's injuries. *Comprehensive* pays for damage to your car that comes from an event other than a crash (such as hail or an earthquake). Finally, *uninsured and underinsured motorist* coverage kicks in when a driver who hits you doesn't have the insurance to cover the costs.

There is a lot going on here, with lots of opportunities to save money.

1. Increase your deductibles. A deductible is the amount you pay before the insurance kicks in. Move the deductibles so high that it hurts. Moving your deductibles from $200 to $500 can save you 30 percent on your policy. If you can go up to $1,000, you could be looking at a savings of 40 percent. After

just two years you will have saved enough to pay the additional deductible out of pocket.

2. Buy a simple, unflashy four-door sedan. Those are the cars that get in the fewest accidents, so they carry the lowest rates.

3. Ask about equipment discounts. Many insurance companies will give you discounts for airbags and antilock brakes. Add an antitheft system and a car satellite recovery system, and your rates will go down further still.

4. If you drive fewer than 5,000 or 6,000 miles a year, ask about low-mileage discounts.

5. Look for companies that want to insure customers like you. Some companies offer police officer discounts, while other companies offer deals to teachers and retirees.

6. If you have a student driver on the policy, she must make a B average or the cost to insure her is out of sight. To drive home that message, ask the insurance company for both prices so that you can show them to the young driver.

7. Don't get tickets and don't get into wrecks. Your driving record follows you around, and a bad record costs you money every day.

Advice

Consumers who lease their cars should consider buying lease gap coverage. For less than a couple hundred dollars a year, gap insurance will cover the difference between what the car is worth, if it's totaled, and what you owe the leasing company. Often, after a wreck consumers are shocked to find that their insurance company will not pay what is owed on the car, but only the car's resale value.

When consumers buy a new car, the dealership often tells them not to worry, that they are covered by their old insurance policy, but that is not always the case. If you just carry liability coverage, you may be driving that new car without adequate coverage. So call your agent before driving off the lot. Better yet, call your agent before buying a new car so that you know what your insurance premiums will be before you commit.

What Your Auto Insurance Company Doesn't Want You to Know

There are two words your car insurance company hopes you never read: *diminished value*. Diminished value is the value that has been lost because your car was in a wreck or because the repairs following the wreck were substandard. There are two basic tests. What was your car worth a minute before the wreck? Now what is the car worth, following repairs? Just by being in a wreck, it has probably lost resale value. If the repairs were slipshod, your car is worth even less.

No insurance company is ever going to ask you if you want to be paid for diminished value. In fact, oftentimes insurance company representatives will act as if they don't know what you're talking about. They may even deny that diminished value is a well-known concept. If that happens to you, show them this page and start negotiating for a payout. You may sue your insurance company for diminished value to get that money back. If you choose not to sue, you may be able to take the loss as a tax write-off. Either way, it is important that you know your rights.

Diminished value is most often a concern when a brand-new car gets in a wreck or an expensive car sustains massive damage. If you have a five- or ten-year-old sedan, proving diminished value is not going to be easy.

Auto

Chapter 5

What Car Dealers Don't Want You to Know

What Consumer Advocates Don't Get

- Don't go onto a car lot and then gripe that someone is trying to sell you a car. That's what car salespeople do. If you don't want to buy a car, stay away from car dealerships.
- On a car lot everything is up for sale; everything is open for negotiation. If you want floor mats, dicker over the price. If you want to buy the paint protection or undercoating, be aware that the price is negotiable. Often car dealers make more money on the add-ons than they do with the car itself.
- Buying an extended warranty is usually not a decision you must make on the spot. Manufacturers often allow consumers to come back later and buy the warranty. However, be careful with the time or mileage limit set by the manufacturer. If you are given a year to make up your mind, you'll be held to that time limit. Once the deadline has passed, you won't be allowed to purchase the warranty.
- Try to buy a car you'll want to own for a long time. A bummer that is played out constantly is when a young married couple buys a two-seater while trying to get pregnant. Selling off the

sports car after a year to buy a minivan is not only depressing but also expensive.

- Don't always buy all the car you can afford, but do buy what you want. Most consumer advocates aren't comfortable with consumers buying expensive cars; they tend to think in terms of transportation, not lifestyle. Not me—I'm fine with someone buying that Beemer, but keep in mind that you can't have everything. If you buy that expensive European car, you'll look cool in traffic but may have to forgo renting a bigger apartment or going on vacation. It's important to pick the luxuries that mean the most to you. It might be that fancy car, but then again it might be some new outfits and nights out on the town. Choose wisely—writing out a car payment check usually lasts longer than the thrill of driving the car.

- Not all cars sold on the used-car lots of rental-car companies were actually rentals. Consumers like the idea of buying a used rental car, believing that it means the vehicle has been maintained by mechanics employed by that company. That's not always the case; some rental-company used-car lots also sell cars that were not part of the fleet.

- You are never going to trick a car salesperson. This is one of the funniest things I hear on my job. Consumers will actually tell me they got the upper hand when buying a new car. Not likely: remember that the salesperson does a deal every day; you do one every five years. The salesperson has his income on the line; you don't. The salesperson has a boss looking over his shoulder and an entire dealership geared up to make money, not mistakes; you are all alone. If you think you pulled one over on the dealership, rest assured it's you who have been taken.

Buying a New Car

a car is often called the second most expensive purchase a consumer ever makes, and that is true enough. However, for many of us it comes in first on the stress meter. We just know we are going to get a lousy deal. But after reading these next three sections you'll be able to walk onto a car lot and then drive away feeling good about the purchase and yourself.

When I was a kid, I saw a movie star—I believe it was Paul Newman—being interviewed, and he said, "We do things or don't do things, and then make up the reasons why later." That is true for most car buyers.

It is very similar to finding a girlfriend or boyfriend or maybe even getting married. We say it's because the other person is smart or kind. With a car, we say it gets good mileage or offers high performance. With both cars and mates, it's usually lifestyle and looks that really attract us.

I will never persuade you not to pick a car—or a mate—this way. So instead I'm going to advise you to find two or three vehicles that you like and can live with. If you leave yourself open to a choice, even a minor one, you'll end up with a better match at a better price (this works with both cars and mates).

If you want an overview of what vehicles are available and simple, straightforward buying advice, check out *The Car Book 2004,* by Jack Gillis (Gillis Pub Group, 2004). An automotive consumer activist, Gillis has been putting out the book yearly for nearly a quarter century, saving countless consumers grief.

Insider Secret

When a salesperson first approaches you on the lot and says, "Hello," don't respond with "Hello." Instead say, "I'm just looking, don't lose your up." *Up* is car dealer slang for the salesperson's next potential client. At most car dealerships, salespeople take turns waiting on customers. An up is the next client. So by telling the salesperson not to lose her up, you are actually telling her you know the system. That makes you an instant insider. Most car salespeople will assume you've worked in car sales, and that can make the transaction go much smoother.

With the field narrowed down now, you need to figure out a fair purchase price. Four good sources are Kelley Blue Book (www.kbb.com), NADA Appraisal Guides (www .nadaguides.com), Edmunds (www.edmunds.com), and *Consumer Reports* (www.consumerreports.org; there is a $12 fee for this service). All four give the consumer a sticker price followed by what is an acceptable price to pay. Since a new car costs thousands of dollars, it's worth spending time and a little money figuring out what you should pay.

If you don't want to go online for these services, the printed guides are widely available and often found in library reference sections. Most banks and credit unions have the NADA Guides available for customers. If you ask, most good car dealers will show you the Kelley Blue Book. The Edmunds guides are sold at bookstores. *Consumer Reports* magazine is available on newsstands, by subscription, and at libraries, and the Consumer Reports service is available online and by telephone (1-866-350-8004).

Once you have your price range, call around to several lots and ask about any incentives that may have not shown up on the other car reports. You are looking for unadvertised discounts, like zero percent financing and rebates. Often consumers will be given the inside scoop just for calling and asking. Why? The person answering the phone is concerned that the car lot in the next town over will give the information, and they don't want to miss out on a sale.

Now you are ready to begin the car-buying process. E-mail, telephone, or physically go to a car lot and negotiate the price. Remember to always negotiate up from your low starting point rather than down from the sticker price. If you run into a problem, get confused, or just can't make a deal you are willing to live with, walk off the lot. By doing that, you have lost nothing. There are no shortages of new cars for sale. You can always go to another dealership or back to the same lot on another day and take a second shot at it.

If things went well and you've agreed on the price, you are still only a third of the way through the process. When you buy a car, there are three deals going on at once: the price of the car you are buying; the interest rate you'll pay to finance your new car; and the price that the car lot is paying for your trade-in.

Work each part of the process separately. That way you can better keep track of what you are paying for each item. Many dealerships like to lump the whole thing together. Don't let that happen. One dealership may be willing to give you an extremely low purchase price for the car you are buying because it plans to all but steal the car you are trading in.

Advice

When at the dealership, don't assume you're going to get the vehicle for $200 above cost. The dealership has a lot of salaries to pay, lights to keep on, and taxes to deal with. You may get the car for $200 above invoice, but in today's world that's a bit like saying $200 above whatever. Invoice in many cases is simply a phony number put out there to confuse consumers and the sales staff, so that only the dealership and manufacturer actually know the true cost of the car.

Once you have agreed on the price of the new car, ask about financing. Many consumers are confused about this, but it's not that complicated. Car lots make money on car financing. They work as a broker between banks and car buyers.

Every car lot is different, but in most cases the dealerships collect fees from the banks for setting up the deal. The more the consumer pays in interest, the more the bank makes and the higher the dealer's fee. Parts of these fees are paid in commission to the car dealership's finance salesperson, also known as a finance manager.

The interest rates are based on many factors, including the current going rate of car loans and the consumer's credit rating. They are also based on what consumers are willing to pay. So—and this is the important part—you are negotiating for the loan, just like you negotiated the car price.

Many consumer advocates complain about this process, but not me. Once consumers are aware of how all this works, they can make this system work for them. By haggling over interest rates, consumers can save thousands of dollars over the life of a loan.

Insider Secret

If you really dislike the buying process, bring along a *third base*. That is a friend or relative whose job is to slow down the process so that you can keep better track of what is going on. Car salespeople hate third bases because they give unsophisticated buyers time to think things through. Instruct your third base to say things like, "Why don't you buy the car later" or "That doesn't sound like a good deal." He should expect to be given dirty looks. The third base can help you get on solid, if not equal, footing with a professional who negotiates every day.

The easiest way to get a good deal is to get loan quotes from your credit union, your bank, and maybe an online loan source. It's easy. Since you have shopped for price ahead of time, you pretty much know what you are going to pay and what you will put down. Call or go online and get the interest-rate quote. Then give the dealership a chance to beat your best offer.

When I buy a car, I always give the car lot a chance to beat the best interest rate I have found and often end up financing through the dealership because it has offered me the best deal.

The third part of the deal is your trade-in. Right off the top, you need to understand that you can get more by selling the car yourself. If you don't want to do that, be ready to accept less than the going rate to avoid going to the trouble and spending the time to sell the car yourself.

To make sure you get a fair price, go back to the Kelley Blue Book, Edmunds, and *Consumer Reports,* and look at the going rates for trade-ins. You will not like what you see. Few consumers are realistic about the worth of their old car. Most attach sentimental value and ignore faults in what has become a daily companion and old friend.

Warning

Leasing a car allows a consumer to drive more car than she can afford. If you are an outside salesperson and need to make an extravagant impression, leasing is probably a good idea. If you are a teacher trying to make ends meet, it probably isn't.

After you have bought the car, don't believe anything you hear from friends and family members. After the purchase, they are all too quick to volunteer how cheaply they bought their cars. They did not buy their cars that cheaply. Car-buying stories should be trusted as much as fishing stories.

Buying a Used Car

The most expensive fragrance in the world is new-car smell. Consumers are willing to spend thousands of dollars for that scent. If you are willing to do without that fragrance, you can save thousands of dollars a year painlessly. It is one of the easiest ways to get ahead in life.

Do some simple math and you'll see that buying a used car is a no-brainer. Consumers who forgo the prestige of buying a new car often enjoy the prestige of being financially secure.

The trick is finding a good used car. To do that, you must begin with what is truly important, and that's not price. Getting a used car or truck that is well maintained is at the top of the list. If you have to pay a little more, so be it.

A good starting point to finding a nice used car is buying a Carfax report. Go to the Carfax Web site (www.carfax.com), and for about $25 you can order as many vehicle background checks as you want for 30 days. The checks are computer-generated paperwork searches that look at a car's title history.

Advice

The sticker price of a new Toyota Celica GT with the premium package is just over $20,000. The same car bought at the same dealership but two years old with 30,000 miles will run you around $15,000. That is a savings of $5,000 for waiting two years. Add in the tax savings ($1,200 versus $1,600 at 8 percent) and you've saved another $400.

Has the car been totaled? Was the car bought back by the manufacturer because it was a lemon? Has a flood ever doused the car or a fire burned through it? The Carfax report can tell you if the odometer has been rolled back or if the vehicle has been a taxi or a police cruiser. The report also includes safety and reliability scores that can steer you away from problem vehicles.

Warning

A car's mileage is an indicator of how much useful life the vehicle has left, but don't be fooled by numbers. If the car you are looking at has extremely low mileage, there's a good chance the odometer has been rolled back. The new electronic odometers are especially easy to reset. Low mileage is not a good reason to by a car—in fact, it is often a good reason not to buy a particular car or truck.

Nothing in this life is foolproof, and Carfax can miss problems, but still this is some of the cheapest insurance you will ever buy. Carfax does offer a guarantee—read it. You can find other companies offering similar services by performing an Internet search.

Once the car checks out on paper, make sure it checks out in real life. Have a mechanic give the car a once-over. Don't try to do this yourself. Vehicles are too complicated these days for an amateur to make an informed decision. Slamming a door, looking for oil leaks, and kicking a tire just don't tell you much.

The American Automobile Association (AAA) offers vehicle inspections, and some mechanics will actually meet you on the car lot. Never tell a dealership you need to have your mechanic look at the car unless you have a mechanic. Here's why: Dealerships know that most consumers say they have a mechanic when they don't. Consumers figure they'll take the car out for a test drive and then swing by a repair shop to have the car checked out. A nice idea, but mechanics aren't just standing around waiting to look at your car.

So set up an appointment with the mechanic first, and then tell the dealership you need to have the car checked. Any legitimate dealer will allow a car inspection.

Advice

Many used-car lots connected to new-car dealerships will offer a three-day return policy. The idea is to get you to buy the car now, while still giving you ample time to get an inspection. There is nothing wrong with this, but there is the danger that you won't get the car inspected.

Consumers are now flocking to buy factory-certified used cars, and there is a good reason for that: they get new-car protections at a used-car price. With most manufacturer inspection programs, local dealerships partner with the automakers to certify that the car is in good shape. The certified used car then gets an extended warranty and often even the perks that sometimes go with new cars: a free loaner when the car is being worked on and towing if the car breaks down on the road.

What you don't necessarily get is a better car. Certainly the manufacturer is trying to certify only the best, but some problems can go unnoticed or are simply undetectable until there is a breakdown. Many good used cars aren't sold on car lots, so they don't have a chance of getting certified.

Advice

Should you buy an extended warranty? There is no hard-and-fast rule. Buying an extended service contract, as they are often called, means you are betting that there will be a problem with the car you are about to buy. On the other hand, if a major repair would devastate you financially, it's good to have the backup. Remember, a service contract is really nothing more than insurance, and you should never buy insurance for an expense you can afford to cover out-of-pocket.

Don't be taken in by "certified" used cars that don't get a factory stamp of approval. Typically those third-party "certifications" aren't as stringent as those found in the factory programs. Those non–factory certified used vehicles often come with squirrelly warranties that have odd rules and strings attached. Some come with provisions such as requiring that the consumer pay up front for repairs and then file for reimbursement.

So what should you pay for this beauty you have found to be in perfect working order? Find the going price as published by the NADA Guides, Edmunds, Kelley Blue Book, and *Consumer Reports* (contact information is listed in the new-car chapter). Photocopy the page with the lowest price you find and show it to the salesperson or owner you are negotiating with to buy the car. Negotiate up from the lowest price, not down from the asking price.

Car-Buying Techniques Your Dad Never Taught You

there are several nontraditional ways to find a great deal on a car. They don't work every time, and they are really only for the most proactive and alert consumers, but they can save you some big bucks.

Look for the ugly duckling. Often a car won't sell because of a cosmetic reason, like the car's color. Sometimes a car will be sent to the wrong location. An example of this would be a car loaded with all the options but air conditioning ending up at a Miami dealership. Another common sales killer is an inexpensive car that comes with leather and power seats and a thousand-dollar sound system. If you drive by a car lot for months and see a car that is just sitting there, and it is an ugly duckling, you may be able to buy it for less than what the dealer paid. Why the big discount? The dealer is losing money every month, and it's time to cut its losses.

Find the price that is too good to be true. Often you will see a newspaper ad offering an incredibly low price, usually on a small truck. The ad is a come-on to get buyers onto the lot.

The vehicle will be there; it just won't be much to look at. It will be a stripped-down model. Consumers will like the price but will choose to buy a vehicle with more bells and whistles. That car ad is a great opportunity if a stripped-down model is what you want to buy. To get the best price, arrive at the dealership an hour before opening time. You will want to be there before the small business owners who often search for these types of ads when buying a delivery vehicle.

Information

I wanted a specific car and by chance drove by the exact model in the color I wanted on a local new-car lot. Since my brother was in the car business in the same town, he offered to speak with the sales manager, whom he personally knew. The car had a sticker price of $24,000. My brother called his old friend and offered to buy the car for $20,000. The sales manager started laughing and said, "I'll get you back for this!" That was not the response my brother had expected. It turns out the sales manager thought my brother had been put up to making a crank call. The car I wanted had been on the lot for nine months. No one had even looked at it. It was an ugly duckling, and the sales manager had just taken a financial bath. An hour before my brother called, the dealer had sold the car for $18,000, well below what he had paid for it.

Find the car that's too good to be true. This is the flip side of finding the price that is too good to be true. Often dealerships will "trick-out" a car or truck with every possible option, and then some. The vehicle is prominently displayed to attract customers. After a while, the vehicle no longer does its job, so it's time to sell it, often at a deep discount.

Tell the salesperson what you want. If you can't make a deal or don't see what you want, new or used, leave your name and number. If it's a used car you are after, the dealership's used-car buyer will start looking for that vehicle, knowing that a customer is standing by.

Information

If you want car dealers bidding for your business but don't want to do the work yourself, check into CarBargains (1-800-475-7283; www.carbargains.org). CarBargains is a nonprofit consumer service operated by the Center for the Study of Services. You tell the folks at CarBargains what kind of car you want, and they get at least five local dealerships to bid for your business. The cost is $190, and consumers I've interviewed swear by the service, saying it saved them thousands of dollars.

Shop till you drop. Play one car lot off another. This works only if the dealerships think you are serious, so be ready to buy. Contact every dealership, either by telephone or e-mail, within driving distance. Tell the car lots that you are taking bids and will buy the car this Saturday. I bought a convertible this way when a local dealer wouldn't come down off the sticker price. The dealership with the best offer was more than an hour away, so before I made the drive, I stopped in at my local dealership and gave the owner a chance to match the deal. I was young and he literally laughed at me, saying no one would sell me the car at that price. I drove a couple of towns over and bought the car. On the way home I stopped in front of the local lot and tooted my horn until the owner came out, and then I waved real big. That was my favorite wave of all time.

Auto Repair: Getting What You Pay For

If you open your hood and look at the engine in your car, you will instantly know you are outmatched. Cars are so sophisticated now that most of us can't read the owner's manual without getting a headache, much less repair a modern car. My father taught me how to repair cars when I was in my teens. Together we fixed things when they went wrong, replaced worn parts, changed the oil, and did our own tune-ups. That was then and this is now.

Since we can't even imagine working on our cars, we need to do all we can to ensure that when work is done, it's done correctly and at a fair price. That is job enough if you believe the results of a California state investigation. The Bureau of Auto Repair inspected 1,300 cars that had been in the body shop. The investigators had a couple of simple questions: Has the work that was billed for been done? And if so, was it done well? The answers, all too often, were no and no.

Nearly half of the repairs came with bills listing work not done or parts not provided. The average cost of each fraud was $811. Although the insurance companies I spoke with denied it, some state lawmakers believe they don't much care what the costs are because they can charge more for insurance if the repairs do cost more.

If major mechanical repairs and car maintenance are in just half as much disarray as auto body repairs were found to be in this study, consumers are up a creek. So how do you protect yourself? Start by looking for a good mechanic.

Insider Secret

Back in the early 1990s, auto repair shops were hit with a string of fraud accusations. Often shops were accused of replacing parts that still had plenty of useful life in them. The industry responded, not by cleaning up its act but by writing new rules showing that car parts needed to be replaced more often. A sweet switcheroo that is costing consumers millions of dollars a year.

Ask your friends, your neighbors, and those you do business with where they have their cars repaired. Do they like the service? Do they like the prices? Ask which dealerships have a good reputation and which automotive chains are considered the best in your town. Are there locally-owned shops that are trusted?

Ask everyone these questions for a few weeks. There are a lot of good repair shops out there; you just have to separate them out. After a while, a few names will keep popping up. Take your car or truck there for repairs.

Once at the shop, don't diagnose the mechanics behind the problem you are experiencing. Instead, explain how the problem looks, feels, or sounds to you. For instance, say,

"The car pulls to the left" rather than "The alignment is off." It probably is the alignment, but you don't want to pay for a repair if it's not needed.

Advice

When talking to the mechanic, don't try to act like you know what he's saying when you don't actually get it. Instead, ask a lot of questions. Consumers who try to fake out a mechanic just set themselves up. If you knew what was wrong and how to fix it, wouldn't you do it yourself?

Have the work order written the same way: "Owner says car pulls to left," not "Realign front end." Also make sure the price is on the work order. Don't go overboard—repairs may take longer than anticipated or extra parts may be needed. Give the shop some wiggle room but not a blank check.

On the work order write, "Final price not to exceed estimate plus 10%." Those simple words tell the service writer you are paying attention.

In college I had a much younger friend whose car broke down. It was towed to a local shop. The place had a bad vibe to it. So when the shop owner wrote out the repair order, I drew a line from the top left corner down to the bottom right corner and wrote, "No additional work is to be performed without written permission." Later that mechanic tried to say that my friend owed him thousands of dollars for additional work performed. However, that did not stand up because my friend had the paperwork. When it comes to auto repairs, paperwork is your ally.

When authorizing the repair, ask for the old parts back. If you see any hesitancy in the mechanic, be concerned. Some parts, like starters, can be rebuilt, so repair shops send those to a rebuilder and pass a discount on to you. It is OK not to get those parts back.

Advice

Another common repair dilemma for consumers occurs when the shop offers different repairs to fix the same problem. One repair will be cheaper but only comes with a 30-day guarantee; the other option is more expensive but offers a year guarantee. Is the shop using better parts or just offering a longer service contract? Ask that question and choose the repair accordingly.

Recalls and Secret Warranties

how would you like to get your car repaired for free? It's possible. Sometimes car manufacturers issue an extended warranty on one particular part of one particular car model. It's called a "secret warranty" because you don't know about it unless someone tells you, usually the service writer at your dealership.

Auto manufacturers hate the term secret warranty; instead the companies call them "extended warranties," "goodwill adjustments," or "after-warranty assistance." Many companies use these warranty extensions as a way of rewarding their loyal and best customers. It makes consumers happy not to pay for car repairs, and if a repair is necessary because of a manufacturing defect, it's easier for the car company to justify the extra expense even if it comes after the normal factory warranty has expired.

Here's how these warranties work: A car company starts getting reports of, say, an oil leak in a certain model. A spot-check of cars going in for service finds that maybe 10 percent of the cars have a leak and the others don't have a problem.

If a recall is announced, the manufacturer must pay to fix, or at least inspect, every car. That is expensive, so instead of issuing an across-the-board recall, the manufacturer tells its dealerships about the problem and offers to pick up the tab. Voilà—a secret warranty is born.

Insider Secret

How big is this? Clarence Ditlow of the Center for Auto Safety estimates that there are as many as 500 secret warranties in effect on any given day. These warranties, if consumers fully utilized them, would be worth billions of dollars in car repairs—dollars that either the consumer spends or the manufacturer eats.

That, however, is the best-case scenario; sometimes the dealership and consumer will have to split the repair cost with the manufacturer. Here's the real downside: often, even if there is a secret warranty, the consumer pays for the repair unless he or she finds out about it or complains loudly.

So how do you find out if there's a secret warranty? Well, that's a secret. But there is a way to find problems with your car that the manufacturer has acknowledged. If a defect has been officially noted, it may have a secret warranty attached.

You find out about these problems with the *technical service bulletins* that the carmakers send to their dealerships, providing technical advice on how to handle problems. These TSBs are also filed with the National Highway Traffic Safety Administration (NHTSA). The NHTSA Web site (www.nhtsa.gov) lists TSBs. Several other nongovernmental Web sites, including Edmunds.com, also post TSBs. Edmunds puts the TSBs, recalls, and maintenance schedules all on the same screen, which is convenient.

Insider Secret

If your recently out-of-warranty car breaks down and the cost to fix it is going to be high, do what I do: assume there is a secret warranty. Once I had a car that was about six months out of warranty when a major repair was needed. I couldn't even find a TSB— technical service bulletin—on the problem. Nonetheless, when I took the car in for repairs, I told the service writer, very matter-of-factly, "I think there is a warranty adjustment on this repair." I didn't lie, I just "thought." The service writer said, "Let me check." He did, and there was a warranty that covered the repair even though my car's factory warranty had expired.

A handful of states, including California and Virginia, have laws requiring automakers to inform customers of any extensions to their warranties.

Travel

Chapter 6

Cheap Travel

getting around and seeing the world has never been easier or cheaper for the average person. That's the bad news. Really! "Back in the day"—seven or eight years ago—serious travel bargain hunters could find better deals than the ones that are out there now. Why? Internet travel sales have leveled the playing field.

Prices used to range wildly for no reason other than the fact that those selling travel services were looking for suckers. A hotel room that was worth $100 a night could be found listed for $300 a night. Those of us who knew the tricks could get the exact same hotel room for $35 a night. The traveler who paid $300 subsidized my room. My $35 was just gravy for the hotel operator. The system worked like this: The $100-a-night room paid the bills. The $300-a-night room gave the hotel its profit. The $35 travelers like me were just an added bonus, filling up what would have been empty rooms.

That system worked for me, but it wasn't a very good deal for most others. Even savvy travelers—me included—

would at times get nailed and have to pay that $300 rate. So, as much as I miss the old system, we are dealing with a new way of doing things. Now that same hotel room will sell at the top end for $200 a night, a substantial savings for the suckers; the average rate won't change, hanging in at $100; and the lowest available price has risen to $65, maybe $75.

There are still plenty of bargain prices, but now it's more important than ever to get a good deal on every single airline ticket, hotel room, and event admission. Miss out on a couple of deals, and the cost of your trip will get out of control.

Here is the most important thing you can do to save money on travel: pick a price, not a place. If you want a sun-filled vacation, don't start your trip planning by deciding on Hawaii, Mexico, or the Caribbean. Instead, let those destinations, along with Florida and other sunny places, compete for your business. Go where the price is best.

Advice

Consumers often decide where to go based on airline seat prices. That is not a good idea. Often the locations with the cheapest flights have the fewest hotel rooms. If all of a sudden everyone wants to go there, the flight may remain cheap while the hotel rates skyrocket. This is easy to avoid by simply checking the total cost of a trip rather than just the getting-there part.

Often I find that flights into Mexico are way overpriced, while on the same dates airline tickets to Hawaii are quite reasonable, or vice versa. It seems travelers often all go heading off in the same direction at the same time. Bucking those trends will save you a lot of money.

If you find some good airline deals to the Caribbean, let the various islands there bid for your business. Jamaica might be a better deal than Puerto Rico on the dates when you want to go. Do the same with other locations. Find the country, island, or area where the prices are most reasonable, and then zero in on the killer deal.

If you want to take a family trip to Tampa, let Daytona and Fort Lauderdale compete for your business, too. You can have your heart set on a ski vacation, but don't set your heart on a specific location. Aspen may be—actually it's always—overpriced on the days you can get there, but Park City may be offering some great deals. Is a trip to Park City any worse than a trip to Aspen? Go to Aspen next year, unless it's too expensive—then go to Sun Valley or Vail instead.

Another big money saver is going where the crowds have just left or haven't yet arrived. That means traveling during what the industry calls *shoulder* seasons, like visiting a ski resort right before the ski season begins or right as the season is winding down. Visit summer locations in early June before schools let out or in late September after schools are back in session. You will save a boatload of money and avoid the crowds. This also allows you to see places and meet the locals when they are not so overwhelmed with visitors.

There are also mini-shoulder seasons. Resorts and towns that are big weekend destinations offer great deals for those who go midweek. If you want to see that for yourself, go to a travel Web site and price a trip to Las Vegas on Wednesday and Thursday. Then book the same trip on Friday and Saturday. The first trip will cost you half as much. Not only will you save money, but you'll also get restaurant reservations and access to clubs and events that wouldn't have been available—or affordable—to you on the weekend. This works at ski resorts and beach towns, and it works best when a location is dependent on weekend travelers. The Hamptons and Lake Tahoe come to mind.

Advice

When traveling during a shoulder season or off-season, before booking flights and hotels, make sure the events you want to attend and the restaurants where you want to dine will be open. Off-season is often break time, so if there are particular things you "must do," make sure they will be available when you will be visiting.

If you are an adventurous traveler, consider going to places at exactly the wrong time—for instance, London in February. The weather can be horrible then, and vacationers dislike nothing more than bad weather. That leaves an opportunity for inexpensive travel for those willing to chance—or put up with—rain, snow, and cold.

If you are willing to vacation in London during the first three months of the year, you will find hotels offering half-price deals, airlines offering $300 flights from the United States, and no crowds. If you are lucky, the weather won't be so bad. That's what happened to me—I went to London once in February, and it wasn't too cold and only sprinkled, and it didn't do that much. I managed to see the Crown Jewels without standing in line and got into the hottest restaurant in town all because I chanced a trip during the off-season.

Buying Air Time

buying an airline ticket feels like buying a lottery ticket these days. Call the reservation line at the right instant and you get a killer deal. Call or visit the Web site an hour later and you'll have to take out a long-term loan to pay for the ticket. It's crazy. I used to travel always knowing I had the best-priced ticket on the plane. Now I am always convinced, no matter what I've paid, that I'm getting ripped off.

Airline ticket prices jump up and down moment to moment. Airlines have very sophisticated computers that are keeping track of how many passengers have booked tickets for each flight. The computer program knows how many passengers usually book that flight by that date and time. If more passengers have bought tickets than would be expected, prices go up. If fewer tickets have been sold, prices can go down.

The computer also keeps track of frequent fliers. If fewer than normal are booking the flight using miles, that means more seats for passengers paying cash for tickets, so the price will go down for paying customers. If frequent fliers are flocking to a flight, some will be denied seats, while cash passengers will be charged more.

Recently I flew from San Francisco to Washington, D.C., on business. The flight was booked a week ahead of time and cost my employer $1,025. A lousy deal, so to pass the time on the trip, I took out my camcorder and started asking other passengers what they had paid for a ticket.

The differences were stunning. I found passengers who had paid less than $300 for their round-trip tickets. On the other end of the scale, I found passengers who had paid more than ten times the lowest rate. Three thousand dollars and more for round-trip tickets, and not all of those passengers were even sitting in first class.

The majority of the tickets had been bought either in the $500–$600 range or for about $1,000. Several passengers were flying round trips to Asia or Europe, and they had all paid around $700. They were traveling more than twice as far as the rest of us but still had tickets priced well below what many of us had paid.

Insider Secret

After buying an airline ticket, keep track of the price. If you paid $400 and the current going rate is $200, call the airline and ask for a reduction. The airline is not obligated to give you the lower price, but most full-service airlines will give you a rebate in an effort to keep a customer happy.

If you have a favorite airline and try to collect miles with the airline's frequent-flier program, good for you, but remember that miles are valued at about 2.5 cents each, so don't focus on them to the exclusion of a good deal. When booking a flight, start by looking at price, not brand name. I do have preferences for certain airlines, but those company preferences only last as long as their prices are competitive.

There is simply too much going on with the pricing of tickets for me to get too attached to an airline. Here's a good example of why being brand conscious can cost you a lot of money for no good reason. A colleague of mine was booking a trip, again from San Francisco to Washington, D.C., and found a flight on United Airlines for $576—a pretty good deal, as you can tell from my previous example. But then he found a similar flight on US Airways for just $258—now that was a great price.

As he compared the two offers, he found that the US Airways plane left the airport at exactly the same time as the United Airlines flight. The plane landed at the same time, too. There was a coincidence. Then when he checked the return flight, he found that it would take off and land at the same time as the United Airlines flight. What was going on?

Advice

An easy way to keep track of good deals is to sign up for the e-mails that the airlines offer. Every week the companies send out their latest deals and alerts; some of those deals are spectacular.

It turned out that the US Airways flight *was* the United Airlines flight. US Airways and United have a partnership, like many other airlines, whereby they cooperate by doing a thing call *code sharing*. That means they sell each other's tickets. So US Airways was selling the United ticket cheaper than United was.

Neither airline was hiding the code share; in fact, there was a note right on the computer screen pointing out the code-share arrangement and saying that the US Airways flight was actually taking place on a United plane. These types of things happen all the time with airlines. Since the business model is so different from that of other industries, it is important that consumers stay alert and treat airlines as a different type of commodity. Where airlines will compete like mad dogs in a feeding frenzy on one air route, on the next they act like lap dogs feeding passengers to each other.

Information

If you want to become savvy on airline and travel issues, seek out Ed Perkins's travel columns. The founder and now retired editor of *Consumer Reports Travel Letter*, he is quite the consumer watchdog. If your local newspaper does not carry Ed's travel column, call and complain. Ed's column can be found online at Smarter Living (www.smarterliving.com).

Here's how to go about finding the cheapest rates on traditional airline tickets. Be ready to take notes, since all the information will blur together by the time you are done.

1. Do not call a travel agent; few will book a stand-alone airline ticket, since they get paid so little by the airlines. You will simply irritate the agent and yourself, or pay extra for a service you can perform yourself.

2. Visit a travel Web site like Travelocity (www.travelocity.com) or Orbitz (www.orbitz.com), and put in the dates and times when you want to travel. Write down the best three prices.

3. Visit the individual airlines' Web sites. Write down the three best prices.
4. Call the airline reservation lines. Write down the three best prices.
5. Make sure you are comparing apples with apples. How long will it take to get from point A to point B? Are you comparing a direct, nonstop flight with one that hopscotches across the country? Your time is worth something, so don't leave it out of the equation.
6. Book your ticket.
7. If you book several weeks in advance, check back occasionally to see if the ticket prices have gone down.

Tickets the Airlines Don't Want You to Buy

Consolidators

Most consumers call an airline or go online and buy a ticket at the going rate. Some shop harder and compare prices, always looking for another deal they can lay their hands on. By and large, though, Americans buy their tickets from the airlines.

You don't have to do that. If you put a third party between you and the airline, you can save money. As odd as it seems at first, it does make perfect sense. Companies called *consolidators* buy seats from the airlines in bulk and then turn around and sell those tickets individually to consumers. To those in the business, they are known as *bucket shops:* they sell only the seats—buckets—and nothing else.

Other consolidators buy the seats in bulk and sell them to discount travel agencies, which then sell them to individuals either as stand-alone seats or as part of a package travel deal. So where do you buy these tickets? Your local travel agent may have some, although that doesn't happen much anymore. Check the ads in the travel section of your Sunday newspaper.

Information

If your local newspaper doesn't have ads for discounted tickets, check out a major metropolitan paper like the *San Francisco Chronicle, The New York Times,* or *The Washington Post.* Often you can find good deals on college campuses. Students have little money but want to travel—the perfect consumers for consolidators.

Charters

There are two types of charters: the one you are thinking about right now and the ones I'm going to tell you about in the next paragraph. The ones you are thinking about are the flights in which the high school band gets together to fly back for the big band competition in Washington, D.C. You might have been on one of those flights, or on a flight by a company booking trips for vegetarians or veterinarians or veterans. These flights are filled with a group of friends or associates who are traveling together.

The other charters are the ones put together—usually by mega-agencies—for trips to hot spots like Hawaii or Mexico. You see their ads in the travel sections, and they offer incredible deals on hotels and flights to Hawaii and Mexico for half of what you would pay if booking yourself. Here is the drawback: If there is any problem, you will sit and wait at the airport until it is fixed. With a charter you have bought a "ticket on a plane," not "an airline ticket." There is no backup. Usually the passenger would never notice a difference. But every summer season there are news reports about vacationers stuck at the airport for 24 hours while their plane is being repaired. Those are the folks who saved money by purchasing charter tickets.

So keep in mind that charter tickets are cheaper but are best suited for students, retirees, and the self-employed who can afford a day or two of downtime if need be.

Tricks the Airlines Don't/Do Mind

Where. Often, you can change getting from here to there to getting from here to *almost* there, and save a small fortune. For instance, rather than flying from Washington, D.C., to San Francisco, fly to San Jose or Oakland and you could cut the price of your fare in half.

From just about anywhere, consider flying into Tampa rather than Orlando, and you can often save a good deal. This works for both landing and takeoff—the more flexible you can be, the cheaper your flight will become.

Day of the week. Go when others don't want to fly. For instance, everyone is trying to get home from business trips on Friday night, so fly out Thursday instead and you stand to save a lot of money.

Time of day. If you are willing to take flights that leave before 8 a.m., you'll get through security faster and pay less. If you are willing to fly the red-eyes—the midnight flights— you can often pick up a good deal as well.

Two-way ticket for a one-way trip. If you plan to drive out and fly back or vice versa, you might not want to tell that to the airline—often, round-trip fares are cheaper than one-way flights. Airlines are cracking down on this, so be ready with an excuse the next time you book travel with the same airline.

Two tickets, two airlines, two trips. This is a way to avoid paying high prices for not staying over on a Saturday night. This only works well for those who frequently go to the same destination. Book airline A for a flight going out on Monday, and then book airline B for the return trip on Wednesday. As far as both airlines know, you have only flown out, not back. Now book the next trip, reversing the order of the airlines. You haven't stayed over a Saturday night, but both airlines are happy because you have followed their rules.

Advice

After a while you start to feel like a secret agent coming up with all these tricky plans. It can be fun, but before going to all the trouble, check out the discount airlines. Often they offer lower rates without all the subterfuge.

Doing the Bump

This isn't a dance out of the 1970s, so leave your platform shoes in the back of your closet. By law, airlines are allowed to overbook their flights. That is, they may sell more tickets than there are seats available. The idea behind overbooking is that some passengers won't make the flight and airlines can still fly with a nearly full load of passengers. The problem comes up when too many passengers show up and then are denied boarding—what is commonly called *bumped* from the flight.

The laws are clear on what happens to, and for, passengers who are bumped. If you are bumped but still make it to your final destination within an hour of the originally planned landing time, you are entitled to nothing. If you will get to your destination within two hours, you are entitled to be reimbursed for your ticket, up to $200, for that leg of your trip. If the airline can't get you there within two hours, you are looking at compensation of twice the value of your ticket up to $400. If you must stay overnight, you can expect a hotel room and meals.

Once I arrived at the gate just in time to make my flight. Everyone was on board but me, and the flight was full. Still, I was officially on time, so someone was going to be kicked off the flight, and it might not be me. Rather than go on the plane and ask for volunteers, the desk clerk asked if I would be willing to be bumped. I declined, saying I was in a hurry. So she tapped on the computer a bit, looked up, and asked if I would be willing to take a voluntary bump for a $300 voucher. That got my attention, so I asked when the next flight left and was told 15 minutes. I volunteered for the bump, got a $300 voucher, and reached my destination within 10 minutes of my previously planned arrival time.

Air passengers have figured out that this is a good deal and are now showing up at the counter and asking to be bumped. Airlines used to reward volunteers by giving them more than what the airlines were legally obligated to provide. However, just as with anything else, there is supply and demand going on. Now, with many passengers trying to get bumped, the airlines are lowballing would-be stay-behinds.

Rather than offering $200 cash, some airlines are offering a $100 voucher. Most are still throwing in meals as an added bonus, but with so many passengers begging to be bumped, there aren't many good deals to be found anymore.

Warning

Whether you are bumped or not, lost luggage can be a real hassle, especially if you don't know the rules. If the airline loses your baggage, you are entitled to be reimbursed for your loss up to $2,500 for a checked bag and $1,250 for a carry-on bag. If your bags are lost, the airline will reimburse up to the limit, but only for what the items were worth today, not what you paid for them or replacement costs. Airlines will also be negotiating—that is, arguing—with you over the worth of the items, so you probably won't see a check for at least three months, maybe longer.

Still, if you want to try to get bumped, here's some advice: book your trip to leave business centers like New York or Washington, D.C., on Friday night. Business travelers are scurrying to get home for the weekend, and few are willing to give up their seats. Since those passengers are the airlines' bread and butter, desk clerks are more generous to people who are willing to be bumped. If that's you, negotiate and you'll get an even better deal. If you ask for flight vouchers rather than cash, you'll get even more.

If you want to turn into a bumpmeister and make this your hobby, consider booking a Las Vegas trip on the last flight out on Friday night. Those are often oversold, and someone is going to get bumped—why not you?

Cruising

There has never been a better time to take a cruise vacation. More choices and more ships are available than most travelers know. If you want to spend $50,000 for a globe-circling adventure, there's a ship out there with your name on it. If you want to spend a few hundred bucks for a couple of days at sea, there's a ship for you too. Prices—at the top end as well as the bottom rung—have never been better. There are hundreds of ships and dozens of companies competing for passengers. All those choices make for less expensive cruises; however, there is still plenty the consumer must be on the lookout for and try to avoid.

The first thing to know about cruising is that travel agents are still involved with the bookings. You can book your own cruises directly with the companies, but that seldom gets you a better deal. So before deciding on an itinerary, you need to pick a travel agent.

Look for an agent who specializes in cruising or the area of the world where you want to cruise. Finding a good agent can be as easy as asking friends and relatives. Cruising, thought of as exotic, is actually pretty normal these days. This year, 15 million Americans will take a cruise ship vacation.

If you choose to use an online travel agent, make sure you are getting plenty of information and a good financial deal that makes up for the lack of personal assistance.

Warning

If you plan to party every night until dawn while on board the ship, and your plan includes alcoholic beverages, ask your travel agent how much the cruise line charges for drinks. The prices can be so outrageous that you may want to become a teetotaler, but at least you will know what you are getting into.

When selecting a cruise, make sure you know all the charges. Ask about all the add-on charges, like port fees and fees for shore excursions. Once you start adding up all the charges, you may find that your inexpensive little trip is turning into a money-eating monster.

Also factor in the cost of trip-interruption insurance. Even young, healthy folks should consider buying it since the cost of the cruise can be high and is paid all up front. If you get the flu and can't travel, you could lose thousands of dollars. If you decide to purchase the insurance, buy it from a company other than the cruise line. That way, if the cruise line goes out of business, you will still have the insurance.

Always purchase your cruises with credit cards; that way, if the company goes under and the ship doesn't sail, you can ask for a charge back.

Information

When booking a cruise, consider buying your airline tickets as part of a vacation package. The flights are often cheaper, and in the event of a war, attack, or natural disaster, you will have an easier time getting a refund or making new arrangements. We saw that time and again after the terrorist attacks on New York and Washington, D.C.

Insider Secret

We hear a great deal about passengers
getting sick at sea and the problems
with unsanitary ships. Actually, it's
unlikely that you will get an illness on
board, but it's still a good idea to check
in with the Centers for Disease Control
and Prevention (CDC). The CDC Web site
(www.cdc.gov) lists every ship and its
sanitation inspection score.

An important thing to remember is that consumer protection laws often—in fact, nearly always—don't apply on a cruise ship. So you must rely on maritime law and read every piece of information you can get your hands on.

Most passengers don't know it, but ships are allowed to change their itineraries at a moment's notice. That means your port of call at Jamaica could turn into a stopover on some other Caribbean island. You should know before booking your cruise that unless the whole trip ends up a complete mess, missing a port of call is probably not enough of a change for you to get a refund. If the trip you are taking is all about, for example, reggae music, you may want to fly to the island rather than cruise there.

Time-Shares: A Buyers (and Sellers) Guide

Of all the great questions facing humanity in this early part of the millennium, none has perplexed more than this simple inquiry: Should I buy a time-share? Talk to owners, and you'll find that they either love or hate their time-shares; there is little middle ground. So talking with most owners is a waste of time.

Most consumer advocates will tell you never to buy a time-share. That advice is dated and incorrect. On the other hand, if you aren't willing to put out at least a little effort before buying, this is not a purchase you should be making.

Let's start with the number one thing you need to know about time-shares: they are not an investment. Typically half the price of a new time-share goes to the developer's marketing costs. If you like the depreciation of a new car, you'll love the depreciation of a time-share. Once you sign on the dotted line, you can kiss off at least half the money you just spent.

So that proves it, you might be saying—time-shares are a bad deal. Not really; that computer you just bought isn't worth much in resale either, and neither is the sofa or dining room table you just bought. A time-share is a consumer product, and most consumer products lose their value quickly.

Information

?

Mark A. Silverman is the author of the upcoming book *Timeshare: The Complete Owner's Manual* (2004; www .timesharemanual.com). A tireless consumer advocate, Mark can be reached through his Web site.

Time-shares got a bad reputation—well deserved, I might add—because so many of the early developers and promoters used high-pressure sales tactics. Today that is just a tiny piece of the business. Major hospitality companies are selling time-shares, and that has changed the business. Still, if you end up at a high-pressure sales pitch, get up and leave. Who needs that grief?

Time-shares are set up in a large variety of forms, but here are four common types being sold today.

1. Deeded, one week. This is where the buyer purchases one particular week, in a particular unit at a particular location. Along with that week the owner gets a deed showing 1/52 ownership in a unit. The unit can be traded for vacation stays at other properties.

2. Fractional ownership. This is similar to the first setup, but the owner buys more than one week—usually four weeks up to three months—and gets a deed. These time-shares are often found at high-end resorts and can be priced at $100,000 and more.

3. Points system. This is where the consumer buys points that are then traded in for vacation stays at different resorts. If you use your points to get a condo in New Orleans during Mardi

Gras, it will cost you. Those points could be used instead to buy a couple of weeks in Hawaii or maybe three weeks during the off-season at a ski location in Colorado. This is prepaying for your future vacations.

4. Right to use. The buyer of this time-share gets the right to use a resort—and sometimes a specific unit at the resort—for a set period of time. The usage can stretch from 30 to 99 years but eventually comes to an end.

The trading of time-share units is what makes or breaks the deal for most consumers. Those buyers who are willing to look for the best deal, who in fact enjoy shopping around and negotiating for a different unit each year, are those who like time-shares the most. Those who like "the hunt" often end up with huge units at great resorts; those who don't like the trading and negotiating end up not using their time-shares or not getting the full value for their money spent.

Warning

When trading a two-bedroom unit, be aware of attempts to trade you down to a one-bedroom unit. It might seem like a deal at the time, since you are getting the week and location you want, but it's better still to get the size you deserve as well. So when booking a trade, always say you "could" be traveling with six people. That's true—you could be.

Mark Silverman introduced me to an owner who lives right outside of San Francisco and owns a time-share in San Francisco. The buyer uses the unit for nights in the city while attending plays and cultural events. Because San Francisco has few time-shares and is such a nice city to visit, he often trades his unit for magnificent properties elsewhere. Once he traded for a villa on the beach in Saint-Tropez. If you buy a time-share, think like that guy and buy property that will be in high demand. Those properties cost more up front but will be much more tradeworthy later.

Advice

Some time-shares can be used only in one-week blocks; avoid those, if possible, since they aren't useful for long weekends.

Although most new properties must be bought through the developer, you can often buy older properties second-hand. Visit eBay, and you'll find dozens of units being sold at extremely low prices. If you have $1,000 to spend, there's a unit out there with your name on it. Why so cheap? Many buyers just aren't cut out for the extra work that comes with buying a time-share or the yearly maintenance and membership fees, which average around $700. Some who buy units should never have gone to the sale presentation in the first place.

I got a call from a disabled woman who wanted to unload the time-share that she and her husband had bought for $20,000 less than a year before. She was disabled, her husband was disabled, and neither one of them much liked to travel. During the sales presentation they had been caught up in the idea of owning a vacation place. I had to break the bad news that there was no way to get out of the purchase other than to sell, and they would be lucky to get $5,000 for their unit.

That couple's hard lesson will soon become the next guy's bargain. That's why buying secondhand can be such a great deal.

Warning

There are legitimate time-share resellers brokering deals for owners, but there are also a lot of fly-by-night guys, too. So when selling a time-share, don't pay up front, and look for a reputable agent who has been in business for a long time.

The Secret to a
Great Hotel Deal

o get the very best deal on a hotel room, you need to know "Finney's Magic Words." In this section you'll learn the secret phrases and little-known techniques that can land you a penthouse room for the price of a roadside motel stay.

First, however, let's go over how hotels price their rooms. Just like prices of airline seats, hotel room prices follow the law of supply and demand. The fewer the rooms available, the more you are likely to pay. The less you shop, the more you'll probably pay. A single room tends to cost more than if you are buying a room as part of a group. Here are the three main categories of room rates:

- Rack rate. That's the price suckers pay. The highest price available, the rack rate is reserved for travelers walking through the lobby door looking for a room, or for those customers calling the reservations department and not asking about price.
- Internet/consolidator rate. Most hotels are now offering some kind of deal on their Web sites. Many hotels also sell rooms or offer rock-bottom prices to wholesalers and resellers doing

business on the Internet or with toll-free numbers. These rates tend to be good, since hotels must compete online for customers.

- Convention rate. This rate can be half the rack rate or less and is offered in bulk to members of organizations who are meeting at the hotel or a convention center nearby. I always suggest that consumers check with any professional or fraternal organizations they could join before going on vacation. If a convention is being held for left-handed salad fork makers and you happen to be a left-handed salad fork maker, you can score a great deal.

Now for the best-kept secret to getting the very best deal: use Finney's Magic Words. With these you can stay in the lap of luxury without paying those high prices. To cash in, telephone the hotel directly, not the chain's toll-free number. Ask for the cheapest rate they offer. They aren't going to give you the rock-bottom price that easy. It's just a good starting point, a way to measure how good of a deal you've ended up with at the end of the call.

The reservationist will probably start out by offering to give you the rack rate. If you're lucky, you may be given something close to the Internet rate. That's pretty good, but not good enough.

Tell the reservation clerk you "understand" there is a lower rate and mention that you are a union member, a teacher, or a police officer. Say you are a member of an alumni association or a warehouse club. Why all this talking? Hotels offer special deals to select groups through targeted advertising. To qualify for the special, the caller must say the "magic words."

So keep talking until you say the words. Are you a member of the AARP? Tell the reservationist. Still no deal? Tell the reservationist that you want the "weekday getaway" or "weekend escape." Nothing? Just keep talking. The more words you say, the better your chance of stumbling across the magic words.

Several years ago, for a special occasion I wanted to stay at a particular hotel in Southern California. This place is nice and offers hotel rooms with private pools. Can you imagine how much rooms like that cost per night? I'll tell you—$800!

I was never going to pay that, so I told the reservationist I was looking for a getaway. Nothing. I said I wanted the escape. Nothing. I told her that I was a member of a service group. Nothing. I mentioned a car club, an alumni association, and a union. Nothing, nothing, nothing. I didn't get discouraged; I just got hoarse from all that talking. Ten minutes into the conversation, which was actually more like a monologue, I said, "Didn't I see something in the *Times*?" I was referring to the *Los Angeles Times*, which has a huge travel section.

"Bingo," the reservationist said, actually using the word "bingo" to signify that I had won, "the room is $125." I got the room at an 80 percent discount. Why? The hotel had advertised in L.A., looking for locals to fill its rooms.

Here's one more technique for finding Finney's Magic Words. Ask the reservations clerk what the "magic words" are that day. Often they don't know or pretend they don't know, but sometimes they will just tell you. I was booking a room in Sacramento once, and I started the conversation by asking, "What do I have to say to get the very best rate?" She told me, and I booked my room at 60 percent off the cheapest published rate.

Going online to find a hotel is a good idea, but take notes while you surf. It's easy to forget where the best deal was, and then all the surfing is for nothing. Check the same hotel on several sites and you'll often find several rates. There is no rhyme or reason for this—it's simply how business is done. One site will have a special deal; another will not. Still another site will be a consolidator with a bunch of rooms to unload, while another site has sold all but one remaining room.

Insider Secret

The easiest way to get an acceptable rate for a hotel room is to buy one of those entertainment coupon books some worthy group is always trying to sell you. The book comes with hotel discounts, including a 50 percent-off section. Not every hotel you want to stay in is listed, but the savings are good, and there is almost no work involved. The books usually cost $25 but can run as high as $45, depending on where you live. If there isn't a book for your area, consider buying one for the city you plan to visit.

Before booking a hotel room online, always telephone the hotel directly and ask if it can beat the Internet rate. The answer is usually no, but sometimes you can pick up a good deal just by asking.

Car Rentals

finding a good deal on a rental car isn't that tough, but getting the real price quoted to you is a completely different story. Rental companies have come up with a vast array of junk fees and taxes. They range from special insurance policies to cancellation insurance and gasoline charges, mileage and drop-off fees.

So when shopping for price, ask a lot of questions and consider picking up your car away from an airport. Airports tack on extra taxes and fees, and the rental car companies figure if that extra expense doesn't bother you, they might as well charge you a few extra bucks as well.

You can look for a local rental firm, but their deals are seldom substantially better than the national companies' because they don't have the buying power to get the cars or the gas as cheaply as the big outfits. That said, compare prices among all the companies, as some will offer deep discounts in an area where the others are charging a premium.

When signing the contract, make sure you understand all the add-on fees, and check to make sure there is not a mileage charge, or at least that it's one you are willing to accept. Take the walk-through of your rental car, the one that checks for damage, very seriously. Those walks used to be a cursory overview to make sure the bumper was still there, but not anymore. Now companies are charging drivers for tiny dings. If you see anything that could be a dent or scratch, make sure it is noted in your contract.

Insider Secret

No matter what size car you want, whether a Mustang convertible or a Chevy minivan, always book a subcompact. Often the firm won't have the small car available and will give you the bigger car at the smaller-car price. If they have the small car, you can usually upgrade, often at a lower price than if you had booked the bigger vehicle. The only downside is that you may get stuck with the little car, although that has never happened to me.

Should you buy insurance? The answer is generally no. Between your current auto insurance policy and the rental car insurance offered with many credit cards, there is little reason for you to buy supplemental coverage. Still, talk with your insurance agent and credit card company to make sure you know what will be covered if you don't buy the rental company's insurance.

Always fill up the car before you return it. If you don't, you'll be charged double or triple the actual cost of gasoline. Remember to hang on to the receipt in case you are challenged about how much gasoline you bought. Some companies offer a gasoline plan, in which you avoid being gouged on the price of a gallon of gas by agreeing to pay some pre-set price. The plans differ from rental agency to rental agency, so make sure you understand the deal being offered.

Insider Secret

Once, a snowstorm caused my flight through Dallas to be canceled, so I decided to rent a car and drive to my destination. I grabbed a shuttle bus and got to the rental-car office, and it was packed with holiday travelers trying to get a car. The only rental clerk without an unholy long line in front of her was the clerk dealing with customers who had reservations. So I got in the long line and pulled out my cell phone. While standing there, I dialed the rental company's toll-free number and booked a car. I even negotiated a better price than originally offered me. Then I left the line with 50 people in front of me and walked to the front of the counter. Within ten minutes I was driving out of there while everyone else was hoping there would still be cars available when they made it up to the counter.

Renting a car out of the country is a whole different ball game; make sure you know what you are getting—and not getting—when renting abroad. Overseas, an automatic transmission is often considered a luxury.

If you are renting a truck to do some hauling or a move, buy the insurance. Your auto insurance often won't cover trucks. Another good reason to spring for the insurance is your lack of experience driving a truck. Every day you have the truck there is more likelihood of an accident, and it's just easier to have the coverage. If you need one more reason, just look at the sad shape of many of the rental trucks on the road. How would you ever prove that you didn't put a scratch on the truck with the truck already so beat up?

Investing and Saving

Chapter 7

How to Get Ahead in Life

There are three simple rules for getting ahead in life: You can't have everything. Keep your rent cheap. Don't buy all the car you can afford.

You can't have everything. That simple statement is what makes one person financially successful and the next one bankrupt. When you look around, you see others driving better cars, living in bigger homes, eating out more often, and wearing the latest fashions.

Taken as a snapshot, it seems that everyone is doing better than you, and it's time to get your share of the good life. However, that is not what is really happening. One guy is getting the big house; another guy is getting the great car. Still another person is buying the new clothes, and someone else is going on vacation.

Most people in this country can have a nice car or a nice vacation. Unless you're rich, you just can't have the big house and the latest fashions along with the car and vacation. It's OK to have something nice; it's just nearly impossible to have everything.

So pick and choose what is important to you. If you want that Hawaiian vacation, go for it, but put off buying the car and stay away from the department stores.

You can have it all, but only one item at a time. Perhaps a shopping spree this year followed by a nice vacation next year. The new car is going to take up a lot of cash for a long time, so think twice before buying, and that big house could make you house-poor for a decade.

There is only so much money and so much time, so pick wisely.

Keep your rent cheap. Low-cost housing has enhanced my lifestyle most of my adult life. After I graduated from college, my first couple of jobs paid so poorly that the companies should have been embarrassed. What allowed me to live any kind of acceptable life was cheap rent. Later, as I made more money, a cheap house payment made my life very nice. It can do the same for you. Often, stretching to get into a home is a good idea for a young person in her 20s; later it is not always such a good idea.

Advice

On paper I can show you why renting is often a better deal than buying a home. I can also show you why with tax write-offs it's best to never pay off your home but instead to refinance and invest the cash. However, in real life I can tell you that everyone I know who is doing well in retirement has a paid-off home. On this issue I choose real-life experience.

Don't buy all the car you can afford. If you can put off buying a new car for just one more year, look at all the money you will save. Buy a car and finance it for five years, but keep it for six or seven years, and you'll really start to get ahead. Remember, a new car is only new for a couple of months, while a new-car payment can take five or six years to pay off. Again, I think new cars are a fine thing to buy— just not all that often.

Saving and Investing: Getting Educated

Investing is not as tough or as complicated as many in the financial services industry would have you believe. Making the process seem mysterious is how many stockbrokers and financial planners make their money. Don't buy in to their hype. You can invest your own money without a lot of high-priced help.

When I was a kid, I played a pretty good game of billiards. Still, when I went off to college, I shied away from the student union's billiards room because the other students seemed to know so much more about the game than I did. Eventually, I did venture into the billiards room and found that all those big talkers couldn't actually play the game very well. Investing is like that, too—don't let the big talkers scare you away from the game.

Educate yourself slowly, and pretty soon you'll know as much or more than those pretending to know it all. Follow my advice and you'll be confidently investing within six months.

1. Read *The Wall Street Journal Guide to Understanding Money and Investing* (Fireside, 1999). It will take you about an hour. This book, which I bought for $16, has lots of color pictures and is easy to read and understand.

2. Listen to Bob Brinker's weekend radio show, *Moneytalk*. Bob has an easygoing style that is infused with information and common sense. Listen to his show for a few weeks and you will be amazed at how much you have learned. His show airs in San Francisco on the same radio station that airs my show, KGO-AM 810 (www.kgo.com). Bob has his own Web site (www.bobbrinker.com), where you can find a list of stations around the country that broadcast his show.

3. Buy a personal finance book. Suze Orman's *The Road to Wealth: A Comprehensive Guide to Your Money—Everything You Need to Know in Good and Bad Times* (Riverhead Books, 2001) is one of the best. It covers a lot of ground, and Suze's writing style is very accessible for beginners.

4. Read the business section of your local newspaper. At first this will seem a bit overwhelming and even boring. So start by reading just one article a day. Over time you'll get to know more and you'll read more, and you'll get to know more, and on and on...

Understanding money, saving, and investing is a process. You can't get around it by handing over your cash to a stockbroker or financial planner. By doing so you'll avoid the learning curve—for now—but will eventually need to know what you have and how much you need.

Warning

Don't fall for the *Personal Finance* magazine covers about retiring young and rich. They always feature a fit, great-looking couple in their late 50s riding bicycles. About halfway through these articles you'll find that the people being profiled haven't actually retired; they have just retired from their longtime, well-paying jobs. Now they work for much less money but have moved to a beach or mountain town, where they need less cash. That isn't retirement— that is downsizing.

How to Avoid Rip-offs When Investing and Saving

- If you don't understand an investment, don't put your money in it.
- Don't invest in something because your friends or coworkers have invested. Losing money along with your friends is not any more fun than losing money all alone.
- Remember that your stockbroker is a salesperson. Stockbrokers make money when you buy and sell, so they often suggest you buy and sell. Keep that in mind.
- Consumer advocates always advise consumers to find a financial adviser who works on a per-hour basis. Good advice, but just try to find one. Instead, accept that you need to educate yourself.
- Get-rich-quick schemes don't work. Even if they were once sound investments, by the time you hear about them, they have played themselves out.
- If the return offered by a particular investment or broker is much better than all the other investments you've checked into, there is something wrong.

- You do not need six months' salary on hand, "just in case." Some banker came up with that amount years ago. First, no one has that much cash; second, you want that money invested and making a sound return rather than sitting in a passbook account earning less than 1 percent interest.
- When buying certificates of deposit (CDs), look outside of your town. Many banks offer lousy rates of returns locally, knowing that consumers don't shop around for the best rates. Shop nationwide and locally.
- Never lend money to a friend. You won't get your money back, and you will lose a friend.
- Never lend money to your child, parent, or sibling. If you can afford it, give him or her the cash; otherwise, see above.

Investing 101

There are few things more heart-wrenching than a poor old person. Social security doesn't pay enough to live on, and many companies offer only spartan retirement plans, if they offer a plan at all.

Many more consumers would invest with their retirement in mind, but they've been led to believe you must be a professional money manager in order to make the right investments. Don't believe that—and here's why: It was the professionals who were throwing themselves off of buildings during the crash of '29. Most amateurs went on—poorer, but they went on. Investing isn't that tough. It can worry you, but it shouldn't frighten you.

The most important thing you need to know about investing is to start. Take a piece of your paycheck and put it to work for you. Keep it simple in the beginning—invest in stocks or bonds. If you are already getting bored or feeling disconnected, hang in there. I am determined to build you a retirement fund.

Don't let the lingo throw you: a *bond* is just a loan. With a bond, you are loaning money to a corporation, government, or government-like agency. The borrower promises to pay back the money along with interest. So you might loan the company $1,000, and it promises to pay you back, for instance, $1,100 in two years.

When you buy *stocks,* you buy a piece of the company. If the company does well, the stock price goes up and you make money. If the company doesn't do well, the stock price drops and you lose money.

Information

You have probably heard the word *diversification* thrown around when experts are talking about stocks and bonds. Diversification is a fancy way of saying, "Don't put all your eggs in one basket." You may have heard the word *portfolio,* too. Portfolio is just a fancy way to say, "the stocks you own." So a *diversified portfolio* is one that includes a variety of bonds, stocks, and/or mutual funds.

The easiest way to invest in stocks is to buy shares of mutual funds. That's where a professional manager buys and sells a variety of stocks, and the fund investors own a tiny piece of all those stocks. A single mutual fund can own dozens, even hundreds, of different stocks.

Since the 1980s, mutual funds have been the single most important investment for millions of Americans, and it has paid off. For millions of small investors, sacrificing a piece of their paycheck now has paid handsomely down the road.

A common way to pick a mutual fund is to buy an *index fund*. Those are mutual funds that track the successes and failures of a specific set of stocks. For instance, a mutual fund may tie its fortune to the Dow Jones Industrial Average. If the Dow goes up in value, so does the mutual fund. If the Dow goes down, the fund loses value. Index funds can be tied to anything, but among the most popular are those that track the stock market as a whole or track a portion of the market, such as a fund that's based on the Dow or the S&P 500.

Index funds come with low fees and management costs, which is another reason to recommend them. Since index funds don't take much effort to oversee, the management costs are usually lower. The less you pay for management, the more money you make. Since the stocks in index funds aren't traded much, they often offer a tax advantage to their investors.

For investors not interested in keeping close track of their investments, index funds are easy to follow. If you have a fund tied to the Dow, and the TV anchor says, "The Dow is up two points," you know your investment is up, too.

Advice

How do you pick a mutual fund? One way is to look at the information provided by Morningstar. Morningstar is a financial services information company that gives advice and analyzes mutual funds. Morningstar offers books and newsletters and an amazing amount of free advice on its Web site (www .morningstar.com).

Load is another word you need to know. Load simply means a percentage of your money that you are charged just to invest in a particular mutual fund. It is like an entrance fee. Some funds charge a load; others do not. If you invest $100 with a fund that charges a 3 percent load, you begin your investing with just $97. Three steps back before you go forward is generally not a good thing in life. Still, if you believe the fund can outperform your other choices by more than 3 percent, it is an investment to consider.

Advice

Put the maximum contribution allowed in your company's 401(k) plan. This is the best investment you'll ever make. Your money goes in before it is taxed— that's an instant return of about 20 percent for many Americans. Your company will often match your money dollar-for-dollar, or at least 50 cents to every one of your dollars. That is a huge return on your investment. So don't miss out on a dime; go to your personnel office and sign up for your 401(k) plan today.

Mutual funds have been getting bad publicity lately because some of their owners and managers have been ripping off the small investor. That matters to you because as an individual you are the "small investor" being ripped off. Although there have been many different schemes and scams, the bottom line comes down to the fact that the big guys have stolen money from the little guys. It's classic schoolyard-bully behavior.

That's called stealing in your neighborhood and mine. On Wall Street, that is all too often known as "the way business is done." There's not much you can do to protect yourself, other than to keep close track of how well your mutual fund is doing and cash out if the rate of return is too low or the management team gets busted.

Buying individual stocks can be more profitable than buying into a mutual fund—just ask anyone who bought eBay shares early on. Buying individual stocks can also be devastating—ask anyone who held on to their Enron shares. Investing in individual shares is only for those who really want to put in the time and effort to study stocks and markets. It also helps if you have a strong stomach.

Warning

Your number one investment priority must be your retirement. Many consumers think it's their children's college fund, but they are wrong, and here's why: you can get student loans; you can't get a retiree loan.

Home

Chapter 8

Buying a Home, and Advice Real Estate Agents Hate

Owning a home is the foundation that most family fortunes are based on. Buy the right home, and your family will live comfortably while you build up equity. Buy the wrong home, and you'll go into debt while your family lives with inconvenience.

Warning

When selecting a home, keep in mind that a good school district is as important as the neighborhood itself. I can't tell you how many times I have reported on new homeowners who assumed their children would go to the nearby school when that wasn't the case. The reason the home was such a "good deal" was that the local schools weren't so hot, and other homeowners were avoiding the house.

The key to buying a home is to get one that is structurally sound. You do not want to buy a home that has a bad foundation or a roof ready to collapse. Often homes are sold in a state of disrepair because the owner figures that any buyer will underestimate the cost of doing the work. Those owners are usually right; consumers seldom can estimate correctly what it will cost to paint a home, much less fix a foundation. So unless you are a contractor or masochist, leave the big fixer-uppers for another buyer.

The asking price of a home should mean very little to you. Often the asking price is way over what the house is expected to sell for and is set high in hopes that a sucker will come along. Sometimes a house is underpriced as a way to lure potential buyers and spark a bidding war. So "asking" shouldn't even be used as a guide; instead, talk it over with your real estate agent. Ask what other similar homes in the area have sold for.

Advice

Don't fall in love with the house or condo, or you'll pay too much. A home is a very emotional thing, but it is also an investment, and few investors fall in love with their certificates of deposit or the stock of a particular company.

When buying any home, new or preexisting, hire a home inspector. You have too much money on the line for you to go it alone. Go with the home inspector when he or she gives the house the once-over. Home inspectors are like everyone else and do a better, more thorough job when their boss is watching. You are the boss, so watch and ask lots of questions of the inspector.

Often a home inspector will be willing to verbally tell you more than he is willing to put into writing. Also, by being there with the inspector, you'll know exactly what the inspector has done. Many refuse to go up on a roof, while others will not open and close windows and doors. You need to know what the inspector hasn't seen as much as what he has inspected. A good source for finding a home inspector is the American Society of Home Inspectors (1-800-743-ASHI [1-800-743-2744]; www.ashi.com).

Advice

You should get a home warranty whenever buying a house. A warranty offers additional protection against the unknown, but don't think of it as an alternative to a good home inspection.

Before making an offer, drive from the home you are considering to your workplace. Make the drive during commute hours. If you live in an urban setting, you may find that the commute is horrible. Knock on a few doors and talk with your potential neighbors. They know the area and have no incentive to whitewash over any problems. Ask what they like best and least about their homes and the neighborhood.

If you are looking in an area you are unfamiliar with—this is true for many who get transferred by their employers—a good real estate agent is a necessity. Get references and interview several agents. Look for someone who has helped buy and sell numerous homes in the area.

If you are looking in a neighborhood you know well—for instance, you already live there and have been going to open houses and following the market—you don't need someone to show you around. If you have bought homes before, you might not need someone to hold your hand through the process. So if you don't want or need a full-service agent, why would you pay for it? Instead, look for an agent, maybe an acquaintance or friend, who will do the job less expensively. There is a growing trend for some agents to charge lower fees if you need only a few services, such as help preparing the sales contract or handling the closing details.

I can already hear the wailing from agents: the buyer doesn't pay a commission, so how could the buyer possibly pay the agent less? In truth, the buyer pays the entire commission. If the home isn't sold, there is no commission.

Warning

In states where an agent is allowed to represent both the seller and the buyer—*dual agency,* as it's called—the agent will often try to steer buyers to a home she has listed. If you have an agent who is only showing you homes listed through the office she works out of, find a new agent fast.

When a home is sold with the help of a real estate agent, the seller customarily pays a 6 percent commission (this fee can change from area to area). The agent with the listing gets 3 percent; the agent with the buyer gets the other 3 percent. If an agent is lucky enough to get both the buyer and the seller, he makes a cool 6 percent.

Smart buyers bargain with the real estate agent before they bargain for the home itself. Find an agent who is willing to take less money for doing less work. Agents hate the fact that I'll even talk about this, but why should a buyer's agent get a full 3 percent when he isn't doing 3 percent worth of work? Instead, explain to the agent that you are willing to pay 2 percent. You will get a taker—I guarantee it. Just remember that the agent is doing less, so you'd better know what you are doing.

How do you get the 1 percent? Simply have the agent have 1 percent taken out of her commission and applied to the home. So if you are buying a $200,000 home, have your agent mark it down to $198,000. Now wasn't that an easy way to make two grand? Tell your agent I sent you.

Getting a Mortgage

The money you borrow to buy a home usually costs more than the home itself. That is the most important thing you need to know. It's easy to get so tied up negotiating the price of a home that the big savings that come with the right loan can be overlooked.

Mortgages are "complex financial instruments," but don't let a phrase like that one scare you. At their heart, mortgages are easy to understand. Put all the talk of "ARMs," "rates," and "junk fees" aside for the moment—we'll get back to them—and look at the big picture.

When you get a mortgage, you are buying money, and just as when you buy anything, there is a markup. Sometimes the markup is high because you didn't shop around; other times it's high because the product simply costs more. It's true with a car, and it's true with a home loan.

Lenders, like carmakers, target their products for a specific audience. Some mortgages are geared toward "hard money"—that is, those borrowers who have a checkered financial past; these are called *sub prime loans*. Most mortgages are geared for the average borrower with the average home. However, some lenders go looking for borrowers who are "golden"—that is, they have a high income and a perfect credit history. In all but the most extreme cases there is someone out there who wants to lend you money. It's your job to find the one with the best deal.

Information

?

If you want to dedicate yourself to getting the perfect loan, buy *Mortgages 101: Quick Answers to Over 250 Critical Questions About Your Home Loan*, by David Reed (American Management Association, 2004). David was a pioneer of Internet lending, and his vast experience comes through on every page.

Banks, Internet lenders, and mortgage brokers are all trying to get your business. What you want to do is match up good pricing with a relationship you believe in and are comfortable with for the long haul. If all goes well, you will go through a series of loans as you buy new homes and refinance the properties you already own. If you have a good relationship with a lender or broker, the process goes smoother.

My mortgage broker is one of my financial confidants. He has saved me a great deal of money over the years by keeping track of how much I'm paying in interest. If a better deal comes along, he notifies me and I can pounce on the opportunity. You should look for a lender or broker to be a part of your financial team. It's not a necessity, but it is helpful.

Many consumers like the anonymity that the Internet provides when taking out a new home mortgage, and the rates can be excellent. If you are comfortable on the computer, this can be a good option. The local bank or a large national lender can also offer great service. There's no one place to go; it's where you feel at home and feel like you are getting the service and advice you need.

Banks make the vast majority of loans because they've been in their communities for years and have earned the trust of consumers. If you have been dealing with a bank for years, it knows your spending and saving habits and is comfortable with you in return.

A good way to shop for a lender is to get recommendations from friends, check with the Better Business Bureau, and then select one each: a bank, a broker, and a Web site. If one of the three makes you uncomfortable, add another one to that category.

Information

A mortgage broker does basically the same work as a bank's loan officer: doing the paperwork, advising the consumer, and selling the loan. The difference is, the bank loan officer represents only that one institution, whereas a mortgage broker represents dozens. It's similar to how insurance brokers are either company agents representing just one firm or independent agents representing many.

The price of the money you plan to borrow depends in large part on how you borrow the money. Shorter mortgages cost less than longer ones. Taking out a 15-year loan rather than a 30-year loan can save the borrower as much as half a percent in interest—say, 6 percent rather than 6.5 percent. The discount is given because the lender has taken on less risk. Less can go wrong over 15 years.

Advice

Avoid loans that come with a prepayment penalty. With those loans, you can't refinance and get a lower rate unless a certain amount of time has passed or you pay the company a cash settlement, often running into thousands of dollars.

Adjustable rate mortgages, or *ARMs,* are also less risky for lenders. Because of that, ARMs start out with much lower payments than traditional fixed-rate mortgages. ARMs float up and down with the economic tide. When interest rates go up, the monthly payments go up, too. When rates go down, the mortgage costs the borrower less. When a traditional mortgage is going for 6 percent, an ARM may be had for 4 percent. A huge savings, but remember that over the years an ARM could end up costing the borrower much more.

There are also hybrid loans that start out fixed for five years and then float with the going rate for the next 25 years. Some loans require you to pay only the interest, not the principal. That means a much lower payment, but the borrower isn't buying any of the home, just the home's appreciated value. Some home mortgages last as long as 40 years, others as little as 10.

So which loan is best? There is no wrong or right answer. It's like choosing between a minivan and a sports car. If you have three kids, a sports car probably isn't a good idea. On the other hand, if your kids have moved out of the house, buying a minivan isn't a particularly smooth move, either.

Warning

For most borrowers, the worst possible loan is one that comes with a balloon payment. These loans offer low monthly rates for a set period of time—say, three years—but at the end of the term the loan must be paid in full. Few homeowners have that kind of cash lying around, and if the market has had a downturn and the house is worth less, they may not be able to refinance. Many homes are repossessed because of these loans.

Most consumers still take out a conservative 30-year loan. They figure it's safe, and they are right. However, that safety comes with a price tag, so don't buy a 30-year mortgage unless you need it. If you know you will be transferred, retiring, or moving up, a 30-year loan often doesn't make sense. Remember, the object is not always to pay off and own your home, but to finance its purchase. You may not want to own the home forever, or you may need quick access to cash. The purpose of a mortgage is to pay the least you can for the product you need. Don't confuse your real life with a movie image of a mortgage-burning party.

Most mortgages these days are offered with a point or maybe a half point to be paid up front by the borrower. It's called an *origination fee*. One point is 1 percent of the loan amount, so a one-point origination fee on a $200,000 loan will run the borrower $2,000. Many lenders offer the borrower a choice of paying the origination fee or a higher interest rate. Both are fine, although few refinances are done with any points being paid. What's important is that you compare rates and points.

Information

I've been to only one mortgage-burning party, and it was held by a 20-something guy who sold his business and made millions. He was goofing on his friends. A nice party to attend, if a bit hard to take.

Often you'll read in a newspaper ad about a loan that is extremely low cost compared with the others you've researched. If you take the time to read the small print, you'll often see that the loan comes with a two- or three-point origination fee. In effect, you are paying some of the interest up front, and that's why the loan sounds cheaper.

If you are truly confused about the whole process and are concerned that you may be getting cheated, consider hiring a lawyer to go over the papers with you. Although this is a highly unusual move, it's better than sleepless nights or losing your home to crooks.

Insider Secret

When taking out a loan, you are
going to see a whole list of fees;
challenge them all. The legit ones are
the cost of appraisals and credit
report fees. A certain amount of
money is spent on getting the papers
around; there is a huge markup, but
since it's less than a hundred bucks,
it's generally nothing worth sweating
over. To avoid paying junk fees,
challenge every fee that is written
down. If the fee you are challenging
is bogus, you've got a good chance of
having it removed with little effort.

Selling a Home

The best place to start the sale of your home is with a good cleaning. No one wants to buy a home that is dirty. So before calling a real estate agent, clean up the place. Don't spend a lot of money; just get your home looking good.

Once that is done, drive around the neighborhood looking at real estate signs and writing down the names of the agents. Now talk with friends and neighbors who have recently bought and sold. You'll find that there is a group of agents—usually three or four—who sell most of the homes in the area. Interview all of them, and ask for a comparative analysis of how much your home is worth.

Advice

Don't automatically pick the agent who says your house is worth the most. Often that is just a ploy to get the listing. After you have signed on the dotted line, the agent will start hounding you to lower the price.

Not only will this help you set the price, but also you will get an idea of how the agent does business. Any agent will show up at your home with a binder full of photocopies of recently sold homes. A good agent will also have the inside story on why each home sold at its price. For instance, one home was underpriced because it was being sold as part of a divorce. Another home sold for substantially more than others because it had an updated kitchen and new hardwood floors.

Information

If you want to sell and buy property like a true pro, start reading the real estate columns written by Bob Bruss or check out his Web site, the Bob Bruss Real Estate Center (www.bobbruss.com). Bob is an author, real estate attorney, and investor. His columns are syndicated in hundreds of newspapers. If you read Bob Bruss for six months before buying or selling a property, you will be dealing from a position of knowledge and strength.

Selling a home is a frustrating experience for many consumers because of how they price the property. Owners often decide how much money they need to get, not what the house is worth based on nearby comparable sales. A home is such an emotional thing that owners have a tendency to overprice. That's why so many *FSBO* (which stands for *for sale by owner*) homes never sell. Many FSBOs are from owners who won't deal with the reality and complexity of the local real estate market. When I'm shopping for a house, I tend to avoid FSBOs for that reason.

After the agents have explained how much they think your house is worth and why, ask for a marketing plan. Will there be open houses? Will ads be placed in the paper? Make sure you understand and agree on the length of the listing contract.

Advice

Real estate agents want their listing agreements to last for six months; don't go for it. Instead, give them three months to make the sale. With a 90-day listing, the agent will hear the clock ticking. If the agent is doing a good job but the home doesn't sell in 90 days, you can renew the contract, but if the listing agent is a dunce, then you can switch to another agent.

After signing up with an agent, ask his advice on how to sell your house for top dollar. Expect to be told to paint it. Sometimes that's good advice; sometimes it's just a knee-jerk reaction. Agents always say to paint—I think they are taught that in realty school—but ask, anyway. You can decide for yourself what you are willing to do.

Once your home is on the market and for sale, listen to any and all offers. This can be tough on homeowners because many of the offers will be ridiculously low. Often those offers come from investors called *bottom feeders*. They go around making lowball offers hoping to find an uneducated or misinformed owner willing to make a deal.

No matter who makes the offer and how low it is, you should always make a counteroffer. It's really no work on your part—your agent writes up the paperwork. By countering, you keep the home in play and allow your agent to tell other potential buyers, "There is a potential sale going on right now. If you are interested, you'd better bid high and quick." You never know who is going to buy your home. It might be that the first low bid was an opening gambit.

Advice

One way to get a home sold quickly is to have inspections done yourself before listing with a real estate agent. That way, potential buyers have all the information they need in front of them. The downside is, you may find something wrong with the house that you didn't know about and—depending on where you live—could be legally obligated to tell potential buyers.

Home Improvement

home remodeling is more fun on paper than in real life. The final outcome is almost always worth the effort, but the process is stressful. Under the best of conditions, you will be living with dust and inconvenience, and if the project gets off track, you could be looking at fraud and terrible workmanship.

You often read that a kitchen remodel will add 80 percent of its cost to the value of your home, or that a new bathroom will return the homeowner 110 percent of its cost. It's not that simple. A kitchen remodel on a brand-new home won't add much value at all; adding a second bathroom to a three-bedroom home could pay back twice what you spent.

Remodeling should not be just an economic decision. This is your home; you should be proud of it. Your home should be user-friendly and comfortable.

When remodeling, finding and hiring a good contractor is more important than anything else you will do. The contractor should have a state license, a good record with the

Better Business Bureau, and dozens of happy clients. If any one of those three is missing, look for another contractor.

Before hiring a contractor, check him out as you would your daughter's fiancé. You are about to spend a lot of time with this person; you need to be able to trust him with your money, your home, and your emotions.

Insider Secret

It is better to remodel when the economy is not doing well. Contractors and tradespeople are scrambling for work during slow times, so prices are much cheaper. If, like most others, you start a home improvement project when the economy is soaring, you'll pay top dollar and often get less qualified workers.

Get estimates and references. Don't automatically pick the contractor with the lowest estimate, and don't rush through this part of the process. Talk with references and see the work that was performed. After you check out a couple of contractors, you will start to see that often the lowest-priced contractor is not the person for you.

Your contract should have a final figure for the total cost of labor and supplies. If it doesn't, there can often be misunderstandings. Getting the total in writing will end a lot of problems before they begin.

Once you select a contractor, never pay more than 10 percent or $1,000, whichever is less, before the work begins. There are two reasons for this: you don't want anyone taking off with your money and not doing the work, and you want a contractor who has the financial wherewithal to get the job done. Good contractors do not pay for materials up front; they have accounts with suppliers and pay their bills 30 days later. Why should you pay up front if they don't?

Advice

Do not change the project or stop the process once the construction work has begun. Change orders are expensive. You should know before work begins which sink you plan to buy and which appliances you want installed. If you don't have the project planned out, no contractor can build it.

Once the project begins, don't let your money get ahead of the work. This is extremely important. Pay off the contractor after the job has been completed to your satisfaction, and before work begins, write in the contract what that means. You might want to write something like this: "One-third of the total bill will be paid after the bathroom addition is completed. Another third will be paid once the roof is reshingled and the back deck has been completed. The final will be made when the job is complete and the city inspectors have approved the work."

Your contractor may come up with one or more reasons why you should pay early. Ignore those requests and point to the contract. Once you have paid the money, you have lost all leverage, and the contractor, being human, has lost interest in seeing you happy.

Moving Companies

It is said that moving is as stressful as losing a job or a loved one. It's not that bad, but it's no party either. Here is all you need to know about the moving industry: it is so out of control that moving companies are urging the government to reregulate movers.

Moving companies attempting to do a good job at a fair price are more and more being shoved out of the picture by pirates in moving vans. These are guys who have been in the business all of about five minutes, and they don't care if you like them or not.

They are out to make a buck right now, and they are willing to hold belongings hostage in an effort to squeeze every last dime out of the consumer. I had a case where I showed up and found a frustrated young woman in a verbal fight with the mover. He had promised to make the move for $2,000, but now weeks later he was refusing to unload the furniture unless the woman paid him an additional $2,000. I tried to intervene, and even with a TV camera pointing at him the mover didn't care. The paperwork was clear: he should unload the stuff. He was a pirate and he didn't care.

A police officer showed up and told the mover to unpack the truck. The mover refused, saying that this was a simple contract beef between him and his client. The mover all but taunted the officer, saying the police could do nothing since this was a civil, not criminal, matter.

The police officer and I huddled. I was talking fast, making the point that this could be construed as a fraud case, a felony criminal offense. The officer was going to go with me on this until his sergeant told him to give it up, that the local district attorney said moving claims were civil, non-police matters. Most district attorneys feel that way, and most movers know that.

So how do you protect yourself?

- Use a big-time national mover; that way you have someone to sue if things go bad. Or use a well-known local mover that has good references.
- Read the contract, and write whatever is important on it. For instance, write, "Payment will be no higher than this amount," and then circle the agreed-upon charge.
- Consider booking the movers your employer uses. If there is a problem, referring to your company could help.

Other things to keep in mind:

- The base insurance offered doesn't cover much, and it's often all but impossible to get the other insurance policies, which cost more but cover the current value or replacement cost of lost or broken items, to pay a claim. Because of that, you should try your hardest to move expensive or breakable items yourself.
- Consider packing your belongings yourself, or at least make sure you get a quote that covers all the work. Many companies use packing as a way to jack up the cost of the move.

- If you are a woman alone, try to fake out the movers by having a friend come by. I have heard too many horror stories of women being threatened by renegade movers. If you are female and have a husband, have him hang around on moving day; it just isn't safe to have one woman alone in an empty house with four or five guys. Remember, none of them may even be from the area. Some of these guys are independent contractors, so even the moving company might not know who they are. It isn't safe to be alone in an empty house with that many strangers.

Schemes, Scams, and Rip-offs, Oh My

Chapter 9

Bad Deals and Rip-offs

lthough there are always new rip-offs popping up, every day I see a group of familiar consumer problems occur over and over again. These are the classics that never seem to go away.

Affinity crimes. These are perpetrated by con men and con women who use their religious, ethnic, sexual, or other background to find suckers. The key to the scam is this phrase: "You can trust me because I'm like you." Be careful when you hear that—the people saying it may seem trustworthy and may be "like you" in appearance. Underneath it all, however, they are criminals who are using your common background or beliefs as a way to get you to drop your guard. Once you trust them, they rip you off.

Cable descramblers. "Never pay for cable again." The ads offer descramblers that are supposed to get you cable, or at least the premium channels, for free. Don't fall for it. Cable companies are too sophisticated to let descramblers steal their customers. If you do find a unit that actually works, and that's doubtful, you are stealing and can be arrested.

Chain letters. You have been warned about these since you were a little kid, and the warning doesn't change, no matter how much a letter's promoters try to make the chain sound like something other than what it is. If a letter asks you to send money, don't. If it threatens you with retribution from God, don't fall for it. I assure you, Higher Powers don't get involved with mailed—or e-mailed—rip-offs.

Diet scams. If someone tells you he or she has an easy way to lose weight, it isn't true. No matter how much money you spend or how many pills you take, losing weight is a bear—that's why so many of us are carrying around some extra pounds. If you want to lose weight, check in with your doctor and get ready for a long, hard program that includes diet and exercise. It isn't fun, but it works, and once you reach your desired weight, you'll be glad you started the program.

Free. There is very little that is free in this world. So when someone tells you he is going to give you something for free, rest assured he is not. The only free stuff I know of for certain is the items I give away every Friday here in San Francisco. I have a news segment called "Finney's Friday Free Stuff" on *ABC 7 News* and KGO-AM 810, in which I give away items. That stuff is free, no strings attached, but even then, consumers must often send in a stamped envelope.

Gifting clubs. These clubs are making the rounds again, and they are dangerous. They offer those who sign up thousands of dollars if they put up a few hundred. Often organized crime is involved, and consumers should know that these are illegal Ponzi schemes. You may have heard the pitch: You put in your money and then invite friends, coworkers, and relatives to add their names and money to the list. As more people join, your name moves up the list; those at the top get $25,000. It works for the first couple of entrants, but eventually it collapses when new donors can't be found or the police arrest the promoters and sometimes even the participants.

Guaranteed loans. Often you'll see ads guaranteeing a loan or a credit card. For those with bad credit, it seems like a good deal to pay several hundred dollars up front and get a loan or a new credit card. Up-front loan scams are common, so don't fall for them. Most times the company offering the loan will string you along for several months and then shut down. You won't get the credit card or loan, and you'll never see your "application fee" again.

Roofing/driveways. If someone knocks on your door and offers to fix your roof or your driveway, say no thanks. These crooks often say they are "in the neighborhood" doing work and can offer you a great deal. Don't fall for it—often they are traveling con artists who will overcharge, will do a lousy job, and may even break into your home. You should always find your contractor; don't let a contractor find you.

Travel deals. Have you seen the come-ons for Florida vacations or Caribbean cruises that offer four days and three nights for just $300? The ads—usually sent by fax or e-mail—show a certificate offering cheap travel, but consumers must act fast and "call today." My advice: act slow and never call.

I've checked into these trips and found that the hotels mentioned aren't the ones *you* are going to stay in. The cruise ships are actually slow-moving open boats that drop you off in the Bahamas. Often you even get stuck paying your own airfare, an expense that you were tricked into believing was included with the trip. Once you get to the destination, you are often hounded into listening to a time-share presentation.

You don't need this grief—with competition so cutthroat in the travel industry nowadays, you don't have to use one of these companies to find a good deal. A "certificate for travel" is usually a certifiable rip-off.

Work-at-Home Scams

y mother says, "Some people would rather walk across the street and tell a lie than stand where they are and tell the truth." No truer words have ever been spoken. Con artists don't fall into the racket by accident; they go looking for it. Scamsters love the life as much as the money. They want to be criminals and honestly believe you were put here on this earth to be their prey. I'm not overstating the case. They really believe that, and because their belief is so heartfelt, they can rip you off with a smile.

They could leave you broke and sick and old, and they wouldn't care. In fact, they'd *like* knowing you were broke and sick and old. Really. They think they are supposed to prey on honest people.

A scam that just won't go away is the work-at-home scheme. You've seen the ads in the little weekly newspapers, hanging off of telephone poles, and on the Internet. I have received thousands of consumer complaints about these schemes over the years, and here is what I know: I have never seen anyone make money with a work-at-home opportunity. Not one person, if you rule out the promoters.

Think for a moment: If you could actually make $45,000 a month with a work-at-home scheme, wouldn't you just do the work rather than round up competition? If you put your family to work, you could be clearing $180,000 a month. *Please!*

Here are the most famous—or maybe I should say infamous—of this work-at-home group:

- Making jewelry. Ads for this scheme say you can make thousands of dollars beading earrings and necklaces. Consumers send in their money and get beads and wire in return, but the instructions are so complicated that the work is nearly impossible to do. Even those who complete the work are told that their jewelry doesn't meet company standards, so they are not paid for their work.

- Medical billing. This is the one that sounds the most legitimate. Consumers are told that many medical doctors need help with their billing. Some of these schemes offer paperwork and computer software; others sell entire computer systems and ongoing assistance. I have never seen anyone starting from an ad end up with a successful medical billing practice. There are most certainly professionals working on medical billing in their home offices, but those people often started their careers in medical practices and have contacts and skills to build a business.

- Stuffing envelopes. When you respond to the advertisement, it says that you can make big bucks stuffing envelopes but you must pay an up-front fee for a starter kit. After you send in the fee—I've seen them range from $25 to $500—you get a single piece of paper advising you to place your own ad offering big bucks for stuffing envelopes. When someone responds to your ad, you are supposed to get that person to send you the same money you just got ripped-off for and send along a copy of the same letter you were sent. It is a miserable scheme in which misery feeds on misery.

Ten Things a Smart Consumer Would Never Do

1. Go to an amusement park without an empty soda can. Often, amusement park discounts are printed on the sides of soft drink cans or bottles. If you can't find a soda can with a discount, check with your employer's personnel office. Parks and other venues often mail out discount coupons to companies.

2. Want fries with that. When going through a fast-food drive-up window, consumers are often asked, "Do you want fries with that?" That is called *suggestive selling*. Don't become a victim of add-on purchases.

3. Make a collect phone call. This has got to be the worst deal going. A collect phone call made from a pay phone can cost $19 a minute.

4. Buy something that's not on sale. With very few exceptions, everything goes on sale. If what you want isn't on sale, ask the clerk when it will be marked down. Many times, sales clerks will know that a sale is coming up and can even give you the sale price early.

5. Yell at a retail clerk. Clerks have it bad enough without your

grief. They don't make store policy; they simply enforce it. If you want to yell at someone, at least ask to speak to a manager.

6. Buy orange juice at a restaurant. It is the oddest thing: orange juice bought at a store and consumed at home is relatively inexpensive, while OJ bought at a restaurant costs about three bucks a glass.

7. Sign up for a free gift. There are no free gifts; there are only come-ons about free gifts. If you give out your personal information—name, address, age, and so on—you've paid for the gift.

8. Call directory information for a telephone number. An information call costs between 50 cents and $1.50. Don't encourage this; instead, look up the number in the phone book or on the Internet.

9. Fly with expensive luggage. Expensive luggage usually has expensive things inside, so it is like an advertisement for unscrupulous baggage handlers. Save the designer luggage to carry on or take on driving trips.

10. Buy premium gasoline. Most cars take regular gasoline, so buying premium is usually a waste of money. Unless you own a high-performance car that specifically calls for premium in the owner's manual, your car won't run better or last longer because you buy more expensive gasoline.

Getting Started: Now It's Your Turn

The hardest part of any self-improvement program is beginning. We all know that dieting is a drag, but starting a diet is always the worst part. So this chapter is all about getting you up and going without its being too painful. Follow these simple steps and you'll be well on your way. Once you go through this list, go back through the book. The more you do and the more you stand up for yourself, the more you will want to do and the more you will want to stand up for yourself.

1. Pick up the phone, call your homeowners and auto insurance agents or companies, and ask about increasing your deductibles. The deductible is the part you pay if there is a loss. If your deductibles are now $100, ask what your premiums would be if you moved the deductibles up to $250, $500, and $1,000. Right there you have probably decreased your insurance bills by 20 percent.

2. Call your long-distance company and ask for a better deal. Don't tell the sales representative exactly what you want; he or she may offer you something better than you had imag-

ined. Just say your current rate is too high and you need a much better deal. You've probably just saved 10 to 30 percent off of that bill.

3. Ditto your cell phone. Ditto the savings.

4. Put your name on the National Do Not Call Registry (1-888-382-1222; www.donotcall.gov).

5. Put your name on the Direct Marketing Association's "do not mail" list. If you register online at http://dmaconsumers.org, you are charged $5. If you write to the association, it's free. Here's the address: Mail Preference Service, P.O. Box 282, Carmel, NY 10512.

6. Visit myFICO (www.myfico.com) and order your credit score and report. You can't win a game if you aren't keeping score. Knowing your credit rating is a good way to keep score.

7. Call your credit card company and ask for a lower interest rate. If the sales representative says no, threaten to go elsewhere. If the agent doesn't budge, go elsewhere.

8. Ask your employer about every retirement and stock option program available. Many 401(k) retirement plans match the employee's savings dollar-for-dollar. It's like doubling part of your income and is the easiest way to create wealth for most Americans.

9. Put $20 aside each and every week. It doesn't sound like much, but at the end of a year you'll have more than $1,000— a very real start on the road to real financial independence.

10. Perfect the cross-body sidearm Finney Pitch. You never know when it's going to come in handy.

Resources

Money and Legal

Banking, consumer information. To find banks, savings and loans, and credit unions that are financially sound and offer the best rates of return, check Bauer Financial Reports (1-800-388-6686; www.bauerfinancial.com) or Bankrate.com (www.bankrate.com). These companies offer reports and advice on financial institutions.

Charities. Before giving to a charity, give the organization a checkup. The American Institute of Philanthropy (773-529-2300; www.charitywatch.org) rates charities. GuideStar (www.guidestar.org) maintains a database on all IRS-registered nonprofit organizations.

Collection agencies. To report a specific abuse, file a complaint with the Federal Trade Commission (1-877-FTC-HELP [1-877-382-4357]; www.ftc.gov) and your state attorney general. The Association of Credit and Collection Professionals offers information on consumer rights and accepts complaints on its Web site (www.collector.com).

Credit cards. Consumer Action (www.consumer-action.org) conducts an annual credit card survey that examines fees, interest rates, and anti-consumer trends on more than 100 credit cards. The business sections of all the major daily newspapers list the best credit card deals at least once a week.

Credit counseling services. These agencies help consumers get out of debt by renegotiating with lenders and setting up payment plans. Consumers should be cautious when signing up with a particular company—some have driven consumers deeper in debt through incompetence or outright thievery.

Credit reports. The Fair Credit Reporting Act allows consumers to dispute inaccurate credit histories and entitles them to one free report within 60 days of being denied credit. You can order reports from all three credit reporting agencies for $8 a copy: Equifax (www.equifax.com), Experian (www.experian.com), and TransUnion (www.transunion.com). A new federal law requires credit reporting agencies to send consumers one free report a year.

Credit score. You can get one free look at your personal credit score at E-Loan (www.eloan.com). For a fee you can get your credit score, along with tips on how to interpret and improve the score, at myFICO (www.myfico.com).

Free money. Every state in the union has an unclaimed property division. They are the legal repositories for abandoned and unclaimed money and property from closed bank accounts, abandoned safety deposit boxes, and other sources. Contact the National Association of Unclaimed Property Administrators (www.unclaimed.org) to find out if you have any unclaimed property on file in your name, or call your state capital's switchboard.

Gift cards. Gift cards are regulated state to state. In some states the cards have expiration dates; in other states the cards' value is protected by law. If your state allows gift cards to expire, it's better to give a cash gift.

Privacy

Junk faxes. To complain about this, contact the Federal Communications Commission (FCC): call 1-888-CALL-FCC (1-888-225-5322) or file a complaint online at the FCC's Consumer & Governmental Affairs Bureau Web site (www.fcc.gov/cgb).

Legal advice. The American Bar Association provides a guide to finding free legal advice, and to finding and hiring an attorney, on the "Consumer's Guide to Legal Help on the Internet" page of its Web site (www.findlegalhelp.org). Nolo Press is a publisher of self-help legal books and a pioneer in the field. There is a lot of great free information on its Web site (www.nolo.com).

Opting out. Register for the Direct Marketing Association's Mail Preference Service ("do not mail list") at the DMA's Consumer Assistance Web site (http://dmaconsumers.org). For information on getting *off* mailing lists, visit the Web sites of the Privacy Rights Clearinghouse (www.privacyrights.org) or the Center for Democracy & Technology (http://opt-out.cdt.org). Opt out of credit card offers by calling the Credit Reporting Industry Prescreening Opt-Out number (1-888-5-OPT-OUT [1-888-567-8688]); it's a cooperative service run by all the major credit reporting agencies. To opt out of most offers for refinancing your home, call Acxiom (1-877-774-2094) and Dataquick (1-877-970-9171). If you don't want to receive catalogs in the mail, you can stop many of them from being delivered by opting out of the Abacus list (1-800-518-4453).

Privacy rights. To find out more about protecting your privacy, check out the Privacy Rights Clearinghouse's Web site (www .privacyrights.org).

Spam. If you receive deceptive or unwanted e-mail, report it to the FTC (1-877-FTC-HELP [1-877-382-4357]; www.ftc.gov). For information on spam-filter software, check out *PC World's* Web site (www.pcworld.com). *PC World* does a great job of staying current on all the latest spam problems and solutions.

Telemarketing. To stop telemarketers from calling you, get on the National Do Not Call Registry (1-888-382-1222; www .donotcall.gov). For information on how to sue telemarketers, send $3 to Stop the Calls, Center for Science in the Public Interest, 1875 Connecticut Avenue N.W., Suite 300, Washington, D.C. 20009, or call 1-202-332-9110. The Federal Trade Commission (877-382-4357; www.ftc.gov) regulates the behavior of telemarketers, including deceptive and fraudulent claims made during telephone sales pitches. The FTC investigates complaints concerning deceptive advertising and unfair business practices as well.

Insurance

C.L.U.E. Comprehensive Loss Underwriting Exchange, through ChoiceTrust, keeps track of any insurance claims you file. More claims can result in higher insurance rates. To buy your C.L.U.E. reports ($9), visit the ChoiceTrust Web site (www.choicetrust .com).

Insurance Information Institute. The Insurance Information Institute is a resource for consumers with automobile, homeowners, and life insurance questions (212-346-5500; www.iii.org). Consumer complaints should be directed to your state department of insurance or state insurance commissioner.

Auto

Car buying. There is no three-day cooling-off period. In most cases, once you have driven the car—new or used—off the lot, you own it and no longer have the right to return the vehicle unless it is certified a lemon. If you are feeling pressured to buy, you should leave the lot and "cool down" before making the purchase.

Car prices. To find the fair market value of a used car, consult the Kelley Blue Book (www.kbb.com), the National Automobile Dealer Association's Official Used Car Guide (www.nadaguides .com), or Edmunds (www.edmunds.com); or check out the *Consumer Reports* guide online (www.consumerreports.org) or call 1-866-350-8004.

Car repairs. To report defective repairs, call your state's bureau of automotive repairs or your local district attorney's office, or visit the Better Business Bureau online (www.bbb.org).

Cars, lemons. Lemons are defined by state laws; some locations are more consumer friendly than others. In short, a lemon vehicle is one that cannot be properly repaired after numerous attempts. The Better Business Bureau (www.bbb.org) offers information and arbitration services.

Cars, new. For online information concerning vehicle performance and safety, see the Web sites for *Consumer Reports* (www.consumerreports.org) and *Motor Trend* (www .motortrend.com). For straightforward buying advice, check out *The Car Book 2004*, by Jack Gillis (Gillis Pub Group, 2004). His buying advice and articles can also be found on the Center for Auto Safety Web site (www.autosafety.org).

Cars, used. Has the car you've been thinking about buying been in an accident or been totaled? If you have the Vehicle Identification Number, you can order a Carfax report (www.carfax.com). Any information concerning safety defects or recalls will be on file with the National Highway Traffic Safety Administration (www.nhtsa.gov); you can also call the agency's toll-free Auto Safety Hotline (1-888-327-4236). The Center for Auto Safety has a Web site with information on safety defects, recalls, and service bulletins (www.autosafety.org).

Travel

Travel. To find out more about traveling in general, look up Ed Perkins's travel columns at the Smarter Living Web site (www.smarterliving.com). For information on your legal rights while traveling, along with good solid advice on getting around this world trouble-free, buy travel attorney Alexander Anolik's book *Traveler's Rights* (coauthored by John Hawks). Al is also involved with the information-packed Consumer Travel Rights Center Web site (www.mytravelrights.com).To find out which cruise ships have had problems with passengers getting sick at sea, visit the Centers for Disease Control and Prevention Web site (www.cdc.gov).

Travel pricing. Web sites worth looking into to compare airline, rental car, and hotel prices: Expedia (www.expedia.com), Travelocity (www.travelocity.com), Orbitz (www.orbitz.com), Travelzoo (www.travelzoo.com), Site59.com (www.site59.com), and Cheap Tickets (www.CheapTickets.com). SideStep (www.sidestep .com) is a travel search engine that compares prices at dozens of travel Web sites. Travel auction sites include SkyAuction.com (www.skyauction.com), Priceline.com (www.priceline.com), and Hotwire (www.hotwire.com).

Investments

Investing. For general advice, visit Bob Brinker's Web site (www.bobbrinker.com); check out *The Wall Street Journal Guide to Understanding Money and Investing* (Fireside, 1999); Suze Orman has several good books—my favorite of hers is *The Road to Wealth: A Comprehensive Guide to Your Money—Everything You Need to Know in Good and Bad Times* (Riverhead Books, 2001)—and a Web site (www.suzeorman.com).

Stockbrokers. The U.S. Securities and Exchange Commission (1-800-732-0330; www.sec.gov) handles questions and complaints about stock transactions and mutual funds. The National Association of Security Dealers (NASD) offers advice and dispute resolution for investors (301-590-6500; www.nasd.com).

Home

Home improvements. When you're going to hire a contractor, contact your state's contractors licensing board to make sure that his or her license is currently active. Also contact your local Better Business Bureau and district attorney's Consumer Protection Unit to see if the contractor has a history of complaints.

Moving companies. The Department of Transportation (DOT) (1-888-DOT-SAFT [1-888-368-7238]; www.dot.gov) regulates moving companies when a move is made state-to-state. However, the

DOT generally does not get involved with consumer disputes unless there appears to be criminal intent. Some states regulate moves within their borders; check with your state's public utilities commission. The American Moving and Storage Association (703-683-7410; www.amconf.org) sponsors arbitration services for consumers filing claims against its members.

Real estate. For general information on real estate buying and selling, as well as rules that govern the industry, check out Bob Bruss's column in many newspapers nationwide or visit his Web site (www.bobbruss.com). Mark A. Silverman's upcoming book *Timeshare: The Complete Owner's Manual* (2004; www.timesharemanual.com) is a good starting point for those contemplating buying a time-share. A good source for finding a home inspector is the American Society of Home Inspectors (1-800-743-ASHI [1-800-743-2744]; www.ashi.com). David Reed's upcoming book *Mortgages 101: Quick Answers to Over 250 Critical Questions About Your Home Loan* (American Management Association, 2004) is a one-stop shop for the most common mortgage questions.

Recalls. There is finally a single place where all recalls are listed: www.Recalls.gov.

Shopping and Services

Consumers' Checkbook magazine. *Consumers' Checkbook* is a twice-yearly print and online publication that is put together by the Center for the Study of Services. The magazine rates stores and service providers, looking for the very best and worst. This is a must if you want great service and prices. One recent edition rated furniture stores, electricians, and hospital emergency rooms. *Consumers' Checkbook* is available in seven local editions. To see if your area is covered, go to www.checkbook.org or call 1-800-213-7283.

Counterfeit products. Complaints can be filed with U.S. Customs Service, which handles complaints on a national scale, or with your district attorney's office.

Discrimination. If you feel you have been a victim of discrimination, complain to the district attorney, local human rights commission (if one is available), the American Civil Liberties Union

(ACLU) (www.aclu.org), and the U.S. Equal Employment Opportunity Commission (202-663-4900; www.eeoc.gov).

Dry cleaners. The International Fabricare Institute (1-800-638-2627; www.ifi.org) has a testing facility and investigates consumer complaints against its members.

Funerals. The Funeral Service Consumer Assistance Program (1-800-662-7666; www.fsef.org) does not arbitrate complaints, but it does assist consumers with their complaints about cemetery and funeral providers.

Telephone/wireless services. The Federal Communications Commission (FCC) (1-888-225-5322; www.fcc.gov) oversees complaints about problems with interstate calling, including unauthorized charges and the switching of service from one carrier to another without the consumer's consent. The FCC's Wireless Telecommunications Bureau handles complaints about cellular service and paging services (same number as above). State governments regulate local telephone companies most often through varying offices of public utility commissions.

Glossary

be-back. Car dealer slang, meaning a customer who does not buy a car but instead leaves the lot, saying, "I'll be back!"

bonds. Interest-bearing certificates of public or private indebtedness, meaning a loan. With a bond, the consumer—the one who purchases the bond—loans money to a corporation or government entity. The borrower promises to pay the money back with interest at an appointed time.

bucket shops. A travel term for consolidators, or travel companies that sell individual seats (as opposed to travel packages) on airlines; those seats are called *buckets*.

bumpmeister. A term meaning someone who is a savvy traveler and knows how to get good deals and/or rewards on airlines by purposely getting bumped from overbooked flights.

charter flights. There are two types: (1) when a particular group reserves and pays for an entire flight to be used by its group members, and (2) when a discount company books an individual flight ahead of time and then sells the seats one by one.

C.L.U.E. Stands for Comprehensive Loss Underwriting Exchange, an organization that keeps track of insurance claims. This information is passed on to insurance carriers, who use it to set an individual's insurance rates.

COBRA. Stands for Consolidated Omnibus Budget Reconciliation Act, a federal law under which group health plans sponsored by employers with 20 or more employees must offer continuation of coverage to employees who leave their jobs. The employee usually pays the entire premium.

consolidators. Usually refers to companies that buy flights or hotel rooms in bulk from providers and then sell them off piecemeal to consumers at a discount.

Consumer Credit Counseling. A service, either free or fee-based, offering consumers advice on how to get out of debt. It often provides educational programs on money management and help in developing debt payment plans.

credit report. Contains information on where you live and work, how you pay your bills (late or on time), and whether you've been sued or ever filed for bankruptcy. Consumer reporting agencies gather this information and sell it to businesses (banks, employers, creditors), which may use the information when you apply for credit, housing, insurance, or a job.

credit score. A number that indicates a consumer's *creditworthiness*. A higher score means that you treat your financial matters seriously by paying your bills on time and keeping your debt load to manageable levels. High scorers are considered better credit risks and are likely to be offered better interest rates when applying for loans and credit cards. The most common credit score is Fair Isaac's (FICO).

deductible. The amount of loss paid by the insurance policyholder; usually it's a specified dollar amount or a percentage of the claim amount. The bigger the deductible, the lower the premium charged for the same coverage.

diversification. Spreading out investments in different areas as a way of balancing an investment portfolio. This eliminates problems with "putting all your eggs in one basket."

dual agency. A situation in which a real estate broker or agent represents both the buyer and the seller in a real estate transaction.

extended warranty. Purchased by the consumer or offered as a sales incentive, this lengthens the time of an existing warranty, usually on a car or major appliance. A warranty is a promise made by either the manufacturer, a third-party warranty company, or the retailer to fix or replace any needed parts if there is a malfunction before a specific required time or number of miles.

factory certified. Describes a used car that has been given a car manufacturer's seal of approval, deeming it to be in tip-top shape.

FSBO. Stands for *for sale by owner*, meaning that the owner of a property is attempting to find a buyer on his or her own, without employing a real estate agent.

health care spending account. An account set up through an employer that allows workers to put aside pretax money to pay medical expenses.

home inspector. Any person charged with the task of making a physical examination of a home, usually hired by potential buyers to uncover and identify potential defects in a home before the purchase is finalized.

hotel rates.

rack rate. The going rate, with no discounts.

consolidator rate. Discounted rate offered to wholesalers.

convention rate. Can be half the rack rate or less, offered in bulk to members of organizations who are meeting at or near the hotel.

identity theft. A serious crime that occurs when someone uses your personal information—such as your name, Social Security number, credit card number, or other identifying information—without your permission to commit fraud.

index fund. A mutual fund that attempts to mimic the performance of a particular stock index—for example, the S&P 500.

insurance, auto.

    bodily injury liability. The portion of an auto insurance policy that covers injuries the policyholder or the policyholder's vehicle causes to someone else.

    collision coverage. The portion of an auto insurance policy that covers damage to the policyholder's car from a crash.

    comprehensive. The portion of an auto insurance policy that covers damage to the policyholder's car not involving a traffic accident (including damage from fire, explosions, earthquakes, floods, riots, and theft).

    diminished value. The idea that a vehicle loses value after it has been damaged in an accident and repaired.

    personal injury protection. The portion of an auto insurance policy that covers the treatment of injuries to the driver and passengers of the policyholder's car.

    property liability. Covers the property destroyed by the policyholder due to a traffic accident.

    uninsured and underinsured motorist coverage. The portion of an auto insurance policy that protects a policyholder from uninsured, underinsured, and hit-and-run drivers.

insurance, general.

    disability insurance. Insurance that pays when the policyholder becomes disabled and is unable to carry on his or her normal pursuits. A disability may be partial or total, temporary or permanent.

    group policy. A single policy covering a group of individuals, usually employees of the same company or members of the same association and their dependents. Coverage occurs under a master policy issued to the employer or association.

    insurance adjuster. A person employed by a property or casualty insurer to evaluate losses and settle policyholder claims. Independent adjusters are independent contractors who adjust claims for different insurance companies.

    public adjuster. An individual who evaluates losses and negotiates with insurers on behalf of policyholders.

insurance, life.

> **term life insurance.** A form of life insurance that covers the insured person for a certain period of time, the *term* that is specified in the policy. It pays a benefit to a designated beneficiary only when the insured dies within that specified period, which is most often set at 10 or 20 years. Term life policies are renewable, but often the premiums increase with age.

> **cash value insurance.** A policy that combines protection against premature death with a savings or investment account.

insurance, property.

> **homeowners insurance.** A policy typically covering the house, the garage, and other structures on the property, as well as the owner's personal possessions, against loss and theft. This insurance also covers liability claims, such as injuries caused when a guest slips and falls.

> **replacement value policy.** Insurance that pays the dollar amount needed to replace damaged personal property or dwelling property without deducting for depreciation.

> **renters insurance.** A form of insurance that covers a policyholder's belongings against perils such as fire, theft, windstorms, hail, explosions, vandalism, and riots. It also provides personal liability coverage for damage the policyholder or dependents cause to third parties, and it can provide living expenses should the policyholder have to move while his or her dwelling is repaired. If the renter accidentally causes damage to a house or unit, the insurance often covers that cost as well.

load. A fee charged by some mutual funds for the privilege of investing. A 3 percent load would cost the $100 investor $3.

mutual fund. An investment fund in which a group of stocks or bonds is held in common. Each shareholder participates in the gain or loss of the entire fund.

National Do Not Call Registry. A "do not call list" set up and administered by the federal government. By signing up, you are letting telemarketers know ahead of time that you do not wish to be solicited by phone.

opt out. When the consumer specifically requests to be left off a particular mailing list, telemarketers list, fax list, or e-mail solicitation list. Opting out tells marketers and salespeople to leave you out of their solicitation plans.

restocking fee. A fee some retailers charge to take back your returned purchase, usually an electronic device or other high-priced item.

roach. Car sales lingo for a customer who has bad credit and probably can't get financing.

secret warranty. An unadvertised extended warranty offered by an auto manufacturer to cover a defect found to be reoccurring in a particular car or truck model.

shoulder seasons. The weeks immediately preceding or following what's considered the high season at a travel destination.

spam. Unsolicited e-mail.

stocks. Parts of a company sold to investors.

stop payment. Paperwork filed with a bank or credit union requesting that a check not be honored.

third base. A person who accompanies a consumer while he or she is shopping and negotiating for a big-ticket item like a car or truck. The third base is there to slow down the transaction, giving the consumer time to think through the deal at hand.

time-share. Joint ownership in a property or club that offers vacation accommodations.

> **deeded.** This is where the buyer purchases one particular block of time, in one particular unit in a particular location.

> **fractional ownership.** Longer-term time-share investment covering several weeks to several months a year.

> **points system.** Where the consumer buys points that he or she then trades in for vacation stays.

trip-interruption insurance. Insurance that reimburses a consumer if a trip, often a cruise, is interrupted. Reasons for reimbursement may involve the traveler being unable to make the trip due to illness or equipment malfunctions.

trunked. An insider's game in the car sales industry whereby a salesperson talks a disliked or unruly customer into physically climbing into the trunk of a car.

TSB. Stands for Technical Service Bulletin, a report issued by auto manufacturers about specific mechanical problems and their solutions.

unclaimed property. Money and other assets handed over to the government when the rightful owner cannot be located.

up. Car dealer slang for the salesperson's next potential client.

Index

coverage by, 103
deductibles for, 103–4, 215
diminished value and, 106
leasing and, 104
for rentals, 165, 167
saving money on, 103–4, 215
car repair
choosing between options, 129
describing the problem, 127–28
diminished value and, 106
extended warranties and, 108, 120, 130
finding a mechanic, 127
fraud and, 126–27, 220
for out-of-warranty cars, 132
secret warranties and, 130–32
cars. *See also* car insurance; car repair
ads for, 122–23
buying new, 105, 108–16, 122–25, 171–72, 220
buying used, 108–10, 117–25, 220–21
certified used, 120–21
extended warranties for, 108, 120, 130
fair price for, 112–13, 116, 121, 220
financing, 114–16
gasoline for, 214
inspecting, 119
leasing, 104, 116
lemons, 220
mileage of, 118
recalls of, 131, 132, 221, 222
renting, 164–66
secret warranties for, 130–32
trading in, 116
cash-value insurance, 82–84
catalogs, 59–60, 219

CCCS (Consumer Credit Counseling Service), 22–23
CDC (Centers for Disease Control and Prevention), 153, 221
CDs, 177
cell phones, 216, 223
Center for Auto Safety, 131, 221
Center for Democracy & Technology, 219
Center for the Study of Services, 124
Centers for Disease Control and Prevention (CDC), 153, 221
certificates of deposit, 177
CertificateSwap.com, 45
chain letters, 209
change orders, 202
charities, 57–58, 217
charters, 144–45
Cheap Tickets, 221
checks, stopping payment on, 25–27
ChoiceTrust, 65
class action lawsuits, 40
C.L.U.E. (Comprehensive Loss Underwriting Exchange, 65, 219
COBRA, 94
code sharing, 140–41
collection agencies, 34, 37–39, 217
collect phone calls, 213
college, saving for, 182
complaints
by e-mail, 19–20
how to make, 9–16
writing letters of, 17–20
Comprehensive Loss Underwriting Exchange (C.L.U.E.), 65, 219
condominium insurance, 97
consolidators, 143–44

Edmunds, 112–13, 116, 121, 131–32, 220
E-Loan, 218
e-mail
  chain letters, 209
  complaining by, 19–20
  spam, 61–63, 219
Enron, 182
entertainment coupon books, 163
envelopes, stuffing, 212
Equifax, 64, 67, 218
exchange polices, 46–48
Expedia, 221
Experian, 64, 67, 218
extended warranties, 108, 120, 130

F
Fair Credit Reporting Act, 217
Fair Isaac Corporation, 34, 36
fairness, 6, 7–8
faxes, junk, 54–55, 218
Federal Communications Commission (FCC), 55, 218, 223
Federal Trade Commission (FTC), 62, 217, 219
fees
  late, 31
  mortgages and, 194, 195
  restocking, 47
  stopped-check, 26
FICO scores. *See* credit scores
financial advisers, 176
fire legal liability, 97
fixer-uppers, 185
flexibility, 12–13
flight insurance, 86
flood insurance, 95, 96
401(k) plans, 181, 216
fraud. *See* scams and rip-offs
free stuff, 209, 214

frequent-flyer programs, 139–40
FSBOs, 197–98
FTC (Federal Trade Commission), 62, 217, 219
funerals, 223

G
gasoline, 214
gift cards and certificates, 43–45, 218
gifting clubs, 209–10
gifts
  free, 214
  money as, 44
  returning and exchanging, 46–48
Gillis, Jack, 112, 220
Givens, Beth, 60, 64
GuideStar, 217

H
Hawks, John K., 153, 221
health care spending accounts, 93, 94
health insurance, 92–94
home. *See also* homeowners' insurance; mortgages
  asking price of, 185
  buying, 184–88, 222
  improvement, 200–202, 222
  inspecting, 185–86, 199, 222
  as an investment, 185
  moving to new, 203–5, 222
  refinancing, 58–59, 192, 194, 219
  selling, 196–99, 222
  warranty, 186
homeowners' insurance
  adjusters, 100–102
  coverage by, 95–97
  deductibles for, 98, 215
  filing claims on, 65, 97, 99, 100–102, 219

Privacy Rights Clearinghouse, 60, 64, 219
privacy statements, 59
property, unclaimed, 40–42, 218
public adjusters, 100–102
Publishers Clearing House, 59

R

real estate agents
  choosing, 187, 196–97, 198
  commissions for, 187–88
  listing agreements for, 198
recalls, 131, 132, 221, 222
Reed, David, 190, 222
refinancing, 58–59, 192, 194, 219
remodeling, 200–202
renters
  insurance for, 97
  tracking of, 65
renting
  cost of, 171
  homeowning vs., 171
respect, importance of, 9–10
restocking fees, 47
retirement
  early, 175
  401(k) plans, 181, 216
  homeowners' insurance and, 99
  investing and, 178–82
return polices, 46–48
rip-offs. *See* scams and rip-offs
The Road to Wealth (Orman), 174, 221
roofing scams, 210

S

sales, 213
saving
  rip-offs, 176–77
  simple rules for, 170–72
  understanding, 173–75

weekly, 216
scams and rip-offs
  affinity crimes, 208
  cable descramblers, 208
  car repair, 126–27, 220
  chain letters, 209
  credit repair, 34
  debt service, 22, 23
  diets, 209
  Do Not Call Registry signup, 52
  driveways, 210
  free stuff, 209
  gifting clubs, 209–10
  guaranteed loans, 210
  identity theft, 67–70
  investing and saving, 176–77
  moving companies, 203–5
  roofing, 210
  sweepstakes, 51–52
  time-shares, 156, 159
  travel deals, 210
  work-at-home, 211–12
  secret warranties, 130–32
Sherry, Linda, 32
shoulder seasons, 136–37
SideStep, 221
Silverman, Mark A., 156, 157, 222
Site59.com, 221
skimming, 69
SkyAuction.com, 221
Smarter Living, 141, 221
Social Security disability, 88
spam, 61–63, 219
stockbrokers, 176, 222
stocks, 179–82
stopping payment, 25–27
Stop the Calls, 219
sub prime loans, 190
suggestive selling, 213
supermarket loyalty cards, 66
SwapAGift.com, 45

sweepstakes, 51–52, 56

T

tax liens, 34
technical service bulletins
  (TSBs), 131–32, 221
telemarketers, 50–53, 219
telephones. *See* phones
term insurance, 80–82, 83
theater ticket insurance, 87
third bases, 115
*Timeshare: The Complete
  Owner's Manual* (Silverman),
  156, 222
time-shares, 155–59, 222
toll-free numbers, 52
trade-ins, 116
TransUnion, 64, 67, 218
travel
  agents, 141, 151–52
  airline tickets, 138–47
  bumped passengers, 148–50
  car rentals, 164–66
  credit card mileage programs,
    30–31
  cruises, 151–54, 221
  flight insurance, 86
  frequent-flyer programs,
    139–40
  hotels, 134–35, 160–63
  saving money on, 134–37,
    146–47
  scams, 210
  time-shares, 155–59
  Web sites, 141–42, 221
Traveler's Rights (Anolik and
  Hawks), 153, 221
Travelocity, 141, 221
Travelzoo, 221
trip-interruption insurance, 152
truck rentals, 167
TSBs (technical service bulletins), 131–32

U

unclaimed property, 40–42, 218
universal defaults, 30
universal life. *See* cash-value
  insurance
U.S. Customs Service, 223
U.S. Equal Employment
  Opportunity Commission,
  223
U.S. Securities and Exchange
  Commission, 222

V

Valpak, 59
variable life. *See* cash-value
  insurance
victim, refusing to be a, 9–10

W

*The Wall Street Journal Guide to
  Understanding Money and
  Investing*, 174, 221
warranties
  extended, 108, 120, 130
  home, 186
  secret, 130–32
warranty cards, 57
wedding insurance, 87
whole life. *See* cash-value
  insurance
work-at-home scams, 211–12

Y

Yahoo Auctions, 45

About the Author

Michael Finney is a hugely popular television and radio personality whose broadcasts are enjoyed by millions of consumers. Michael's reporting has exposed scams, uncovered government wrongdoing and forced major corporations to change their consumer unfriendly ways.

Throughout his 25 year broadcast career, Michael has recovered millions of dollars for consumers, led the charge for crucial product recalls, and brought conmen to justice.

Michael has been honored by The National Association of Consumer Advocates, Consumer Action, and The Foundation for Taxpayer and Consumer Rights. He has received dozens of journalism awards from various press clubs, broadcast associations, and news organizations including an Emmy and Golden Microphone.

Michael lives in San Francisco.

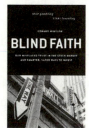